D1326018

N. N.

VOICES OF THE OLD FIRM

VOICES
OF THE
OLD FIRM

Stephen Walsh

MAINSTREAM
PUBLISHING
EDINBURGH AND LONDON

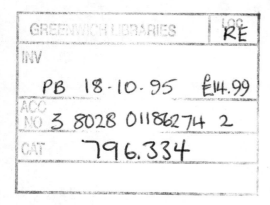
Copyright © Stephen Walsh

The moral right of the author has been asserted

First published in Great Britain in 1995 by
MAINSTREAM PUBLISHING COMPANY (EDINBURGH) LTD
7 Albany Street
Edinburgh EH1 3UG

ISBN 1 85158 713 6

A catalogue record for this book is available from the British Library

Typeset in Janson by Saxon Graphics Ltd, Derby

Printed and bound in Great Britain by Butler & Tanner Ltd, Frome

For my son, Jim

I'd walk a million miles . . .

CONTENTS

ACKNOWLEDGEMENTS

The five-bobs will tell you good players can play with anybody. That is not so. It's like Frank Sinatra. If he sings at the Albert Hall with Nelson Riddle then even if he's 77 you still feel he's not a bad singer. If he sings with Joe Bloggs at the Plaza then you think he ought to chuck it.

Alec Willoughby

Lots of people helped in lots of ways. All of them were good players. Keeping goal were the aged parents, who offered bed and board even when the old homestead was looking like Emergency Ward Ten. Solid at the back were all those friends who gave generously of their time to talk me through the bad times. Creative in midfield were John Thomson, who took over some interviewing, and Alison Rusted, who produced the Radio Five Live series. Up front were all those who helped with contributions from the treasury of their memories; it was good to talk to you.

Many of the contributors pointed me towards others, for which I thank them over again; and many other people too numerous to mention offered me tip-offs or snippets of info which were most helpful. As far as the bookshelf goes, I most frequently consulted works by Robert McElroy, Tom Campbell and Pat Woods, Eugene MacBride and Martin O'Connor, Neil McDermott and Bill Murray. I am much in debt to the painstakingly accurate work many of them have done, in comparison with which this type of book is an impressionistic breeze. No Old Firm book is complete without a nod of thanks to the staff of the Mitchell Library, Glasgow. The books are good but the pie and beans in the basement are fantastic.

Stephen Walsh
July 1995

9

INTRODUCTION

This book is a history of the Old Firm, of Celtic and Rangers, in the 50 years since the end of the Second World War. It is a history of that period of the clubs' football told in the words of those who can say, in one way or another, 'I was there'. Most histories of these clubs focus almost exclusively on the actions that take place on the field of dreams, on that grass rectangle of 130 by 100 yards. 'I was there', in those books, means 'I played'. In this history of the clubs, however, 'I was there' can mean all sorts of things. It can mean 'I played', yes, but it also means 'I stood on the terraces', 'I sat in the stand', 'I watched on the telly', 'I listened to the wireless' and – in one or two exceptional cases – 'I was in jail at the time'. In other words this history gives as much, if not more, space to the twenty or fifty or hundred thousand people who stood and watched, as to the 11 men who were out there clad in cotton or nylon and doing the business on the park.

'Stood and watched' sounds like a passive activity. It should go without saying by now that this is not so. The last few years, with the rise of the fanzine movement, the arrival of Football Supporters' Associations in Scotland and elsewhere, and with vivid demonstrations of fan power, have shown that football supporters are not sheep. Glasgow football fans have long been amongst the least white and woolly. Fans' accounts of the 1940s repeatedly talk of the 'buzz' of activity in the huge, milling crowds of the time. The 1950s saw the busy organisation of travel clubs. The 1960s and 1970s spawned a tradition of inventive song-making. The 1970s and 1980s were touched by sometimes spontaneous, sometimes organised expressions of violent discontent. In the 1990s fan-power has seen off the dynastic families who had mismanaged Celtic. For 'stood and watched' read 'participated'; fans have a much more significant role in the whole that is the football experience than the word 'supporters' suggests.

As Chapter One, *Devotion*, shows, some of the fans who feature in the book have made football the centre of their existences. The book is not a freak-show, however. Most of the fans who were interviewed for this book just enjoy football, even if they enjoy it more than most human beings. Most realise it is just a game, even if it's also the only game, the absolute game. Watching football, for most, is an emotional experience. One talks of a father who only ever demonstrated joy when he saw a Celtic goal; another of a grandfather who was more involved in the lives of his Rangers heroes than in the lives of his own family. Few behave as extremely as that, but all the fans in the book have experienced joy and sorrow, fear and loathing, pain and pleasure while watching football. As a result most remember what happened on the field better than the players who were on the field do; many, one senses, care at a deeper level than the players do. Only supporters have to pay to participate.

The fans who have participated in this book are worth listening to for other reasons, too. They are in some ways – without wishing to sound too pretentious – the voice of Glasgow over the last 50 years. They are not all working-class people by any means, though football-following has, of course, been an essential part of working-class life in the city for 100 years. Many of the things they describe are, you sense, almost unique to Glasgow – fathers calling to their sons down on the back green, a result coming by word of mouth up the street, the survival, to the present day, of the ritual of work-pub-game. Of course, it goes without saying that Glasgow fans talk a better game than the inhabitants of most other cities; there's a richness of language and expression not found everywhere.

The fans, however, are not the only people in this book; the players are here too, and they add their tales and recollections to the tales of the supporters. One of the interesting things about Glasgow players, particularly in the past, is that so many of them are Glasgow, or West of Scotland, men and were therefore born into the tradition of the Celtic–Rangers rivalry. People like Alec Willoughby and Charlie Gallagher were only too aware, when they pulled on the royal blue or the green and white hoops, of whom they, as players, were representing. Players like these talk as fans as well as players; they talk as 'jersey' players, players who understand what the clubs mean, players who feel what the fans feel when the team wins or loses. They too are true Glasgow voices; voices of the Old Firm.

So what's so special about the Old Firm? Not, at present, the quality of the football, that's for sure. There is still plenty of excitement about, of course – plenty of action, plenty of aggro, plenty of atmosphere and a few goals. Some of the players would have found themselves involved in any era. But the men and women, the fans and players who have contributed to this book are more or less unanimous in declaring that what they are seeing from what used to be terraces is not necessarily football of world-class. Witness Brian Laudrup: in Florence a regular substitute, in Scotland an irregular talent.

In the half-decade leading up to their Cup win of 1995 Celtic had reminders of their reduced status every time Cup finals or League deciders went by without them. Their fans were left out in the cold, with only their history to keep out the chill of humiliation. For Rangers, the joys of dominating the Scottish League in the same period have been diluted by their inability to transfer that domination on to the European stage in any sustained way. Defeats in Sofia and Athens to good but scarcely world-beating sides in recent seasons have left Rangers supporters squirming with the unease of a big fish increasingly aware that the expanse of water it rules is the size of a small pond – and shrinking.

So what's so special about the Old Firm? The 'unique atmosphere' (copyright for this phrase goes to practically any media pundit you want to mention) of an Old Firm match? It's true there is a frightening and exhilarating intensity in the crowd at such occasions. In fact, it's an intensity few enjoy. The players find such matches adrenalin-activating but overcharged. Supporters' nails get bitten to the quick; it matters so much to win that even with the game in the bag, no rest can ever be assured. (5–0 up with two minutes to go. But what if a fog comes down?') But this is surely an emotion which is replicated all over the world, anywhere that two halves of a city take each other on. Far from being unique, the noise of ritual hatred in Glasgow sounds no different from the noise generated by a Channel-4 Lazio-Roma derby. Up there on the steep banking of the Stadio Olympico, someone's down to the cuticles and saying to himself, '5–0 up with two minutes to go, but . . .'

In fact what is special about the Old Firm does lie in the two areas touched on above; in the clubs' footballing achievements and in the peculiar nature of the rivalry that separates the blue and the green. It's true that at present Scottish football is at a low ebb; but it's perhaps also true that what we are now doing is performing in proportion to Scotland's size. Both Rangers and Celtic fans have an awareness of history; and their mutual history is one of which they should be proud. The achievements of the past are, for such a teeny-weeny part of the world, pretty large-scale.

If European success is the measure, the Old Firm can hold its head up; between them they have two European wins, three losing finals and several semi-finals. In one week in 1967 Glasgow came close to pulling off a double of European Cup and Cup-Winners' Cup that would have put the city in the Milan class; fans remember with affection a night in 1972 when the city hosted sell-out semi-finals in both competitions on the same evening. The present dilution of quality, then, is a reason for highlighting the quality of the past, for reliving that particularly wonderful era. Whatever David Murray's Rangers and Fergus McCann's Celtic manage to do in Europe in the coming years, times have changed and the chances are that the city will not beat with the same innocent, excited pulse again.

And there is something particular about the nature of the rivalry, whatever other significant enmities might exist around the world. The difference lies not in the intensity with which the rivalry is felt, but in the complexity of the elements that lie behind the feeling. All rivalries have a historical or a cultural or a tribal root; but in no other place is there such a weight, such a deeply complex combination of the cultural, the historical and the quasi-religious. The tribal instincts of Briton and Celt, the blood-stained history of a divided Ireland and the religious opposition, coloured by both of these other elements, of Catholic and Protestant – that's some baggage to take to a football match with you.

In few other places are the differences between the behaviour of the supporters so intensified, so strictly upheld. Differences of look, of hair-colouring, of name, are intensified by a differentiation, down to the smallest detail, in the culture of the supporters. The two sets of supporters have created styles of their own and claim them to be uniquely their own; which way you walk to the stadium, what songs you sing, how you hold a scarf – all these things tell tales about you, say which side you're from. There is, it seems, an extraordinarily sharp division between one side of the city and the other.

Yet – as almost all the fans I talked to said at one time or another – they have no personal hatred for those on the other side. Glasgow is not ghettoised; work-places are not segregated; there are Rangers pubs and Celtic houses but both sides drink in most. Apart from schools, the football grounds are the only places that real segregation exists. Something that outsiders often fail to understand is that the hatred that appears at an Old Firm derby on a Saturday is not a way of life from Monday to Friday; of course there are separations, there are behavioural differences, there are those who are interested in preserving such differences; but the tribal line-up is a curious, split-personality phenomenon. It, and its attendant bigotry and intolerance, is explored more fully in Chapter Eleven, *Rivalry*.

What lies between *Devotion* and *Rivalry*? There are nine more chapters, mainly made up of memories, yarns, recollections and stories. I hope most of them are true. Some will have inaccurate statistics (crowd numbers, perhaps even scores) in them; some will no doubt have been exaggerated in the telling, especially those tales which were not being told for the first time; some supporters' stories may well come from a pool of common myth. I don't feel that this makes the stories untrue; but it is a warning that the oral history on offer here is in some places anecdotal and in a few apocryphal.

The chapters fall into two categories. Five of the chapters (Two, Four, Six, Eight and Ten) cover a separate decade of 'on the park' activities. 'On the park' is interpreted broadly. In these sections the players' and the supporters' memories are interwoven in an attempt to offer the 'whole story' of the football side of things. The intervening chapters look at topics close to fans' hearts, surveying them across the decades. They are linked thematically to the decades they sit beside; Chapter Three, *Crowds*, has its starting-point in the post-war boom in attendances but surveys the look and conduct of crowds up to the present. Chapter Five, *Travel*, rises similarly from the growth of awaydays in the 1950s; *Songs* (Chapter Seven) springs from the outpourings of the Beatlemania era; and Chapter Nine, *Trouble*, is, inevitably, tied in with the decade that brought you the Hampden Riot. These chapters can only suggest the rich life that following football has been, especially at times other than the present; at times when crowds were huge, when crowds stood up, when clubs saw crowds as a living animal and not just a marketable blob to sell replica shirts to.

It may mean that it has one foot stuck irretrievably in the past, but if there is just one theme running through the book it's a, perhaps naïve, enthusiasm for how things were and a, perhaps naïve, antagonism towards how things are turning out in the brave new world of football as commerce. Manchester United now have more people peddling their goodies than they have involved in the business of peddling on-the-pitch dreams. Rangers are already well on their way down the same road and Celtic will wish to follow on as fast as their historically unbusiness-like legs can carry them. No one's suggesting they don't need money. But in moving too aggressively in the commercial direction they run the huge risk of losing sight of the community sense and link that created and nourished them. It's that community sense that these voices of the Old Firm speak of most vividly, reminding the objects of their passion, be they in blue and white or green and white, that football clubs belong, in a far more significant way than the financial, to their supporters.

LIST OF
INTERVIEWEES

Celtic players

Johnny Bonnar
Denis Connaghan
Sean Fallon
Charlie Gallagher
Tommy Gemmell
Davie Hay
John Hughes
Matt Lynch
Mick McCarthy
Danny McGrain
Murdo MacLeod
Billy McNeill
John McPhail
Johnny Paton

Rangers players

Doug Baillie
Terry Butcher
Sandy Clark
Richard Gough
John Greig
Johnny Hubbard
Willie Johnston
Ian McColl
Alec Willoughby
Alex MacDonald
David McKinnon
Alex Miller
Jimmy Nicholl

Billy Ritchie
Jock Shaw
Gordon Smith

Celtic supporters

John Butterfield
Andy Cottingham
Gerry Devlin
Margaret Devlin
James Dunbar
Hugh Ferrie
Jimmy Finnis
Steven Gall
Frank Glencross
Tony Griffin
Tommy Hyndman
John Larkin
John Lawson
Brian McBride
Eugene MacBride
Neil McDermott
Jim MacDonald
Eddie McGraw
Liam MacLuskey
Mick Maher
George Moore
Frank Mooty
Gerry Mulvenna
Seamus Murphy
Dominic Murray
Stephen Murray

David Potter
Jack Prior
George Sheridan
Joe Shevlin
Adam Shiels
John Thomson
Hugh Toner

Rangers supporters

Susan Ambrose
Harvey Beaton
Alex Bell
Jimmy Brown
Jim Cooke
Brian Craig
Stuart Daniels
Dougie Dick
Scot Dickson
Mark Dingwall
Alan Galloway

John Gardner
Colin Glass
Gordon Inglis
Jack Jardine
Stef Jardine
William Johnston
Bill Lamond
Colin Lamond
Sandra Lewsey
Charlie Logan
Bill McArthur
George MacLeod
Robert Malcolm
David Palmer
Iain Patterson
Andy Robertson
John Slowey
John Watson
Leslie White

Chapter One

DEVOTION

The Old Firm occupies a curious position in the minds of Scottish football followers. To some Old Firm fans – particularly those who work in Scottish broadcasting – there seems to be not much of interest in Scottish football beyond the Old Firm. To non-Old Firm fans – and this is something that the attitude of broadcasters has much to do with – the Old Firm is a monster which gobbles up an undue share of attention and permanently casts a long shadow over the aspirations and achievements of the nation's other teams.

Old Firm fans find themselves in a bit of a bind. They follow teams with some clout, which is good, because, as supporters they want their teams to win things. But the ultimate index of loyal support is supporting a team that doesn't win anything, and Old Firm fans can't prove their loyalty by staying true through endless years of barren trophylessness in the way that a Hearts or a St Johnstone fan can. What's worse is that as soon as bad times come and crowds go down (as they do everywhere in bad times) it's 'proved' to all other mobs that Rangers and Celtic fans are just fairweathers and glory-hunters.

Many Old Firm fans are obsessed with statistics, and particularly with crowd numbers; the obsession is to refute the mockery, to show that they are true fans; or, if not true in the sense that a St Mirren fan might understand it, at least truer than the other side. Old Firm fans do express a deep and obsessive commitment to their clubs. Ignore the camel coats, the flesh-squeezing in the hospitality boxes and the slick-suited chairmen, they plead, and see us for football fans, just like you. Of course to the outsiders, this cuts no mustard whatsoever; Old Firm fans pay their tribute to the monster in their season-ticket fees.

'Rangers fans are loyal, Celtic fans are faithful' – so goes the saying. It's a sentence that says a lot about them. They cannot bring themselves to use the same word to describe themselves. Loyal is Protestant, church, Ulster; faithful is Catholic, chapel, Ireland. But they do, after all, share something – they are fans too. They share a single-minded devotion to their teams which is not unique, but is at least special and which runs from the cradle to the grave.

WILLIAM JOHNSTON   My kid's just two. Five or six months ago he could already sing 'The Billy Boys'. He's never seen Rangers but that doesn't matter. He's going to be a Rangers fan – because his dad's a Rangers fan.

SEAMUS MURPHY   I was born in London but brought up in Glasgow; in 1943 – I was seven – my mother abandoned me and my baby brother. We were sent to Castlemilk Orphanage; this was in the days before the scheme was built. The boys were all Celtic supporters; we spent our days eating, sleeping, talking and playing football. And we were always singing: 'Delaney in the centre, the ball was in the net, and there was Jerry Dawson, a-lying in the wet.' I remember one Christmas we were taken to the Kelvin Hall to see the circus, a special show for all the orphanages in the Glasgow area. One of the acts was two teams of dogs playing football; one side was in green and white, the other was in blue. When the greens scored a big cheer went up; but it did when the blues scored, too.

IAIN PATTERSON   Why do people support Rangers? A lot of it has been handed down through families. Possibly the best example of this is Alan Spence in his book *The Colours They Are Fine* – where he talks about how his grandfather and father gave him talks about Rangers players and the legends associated with them. He says that although he heard them hundreds of times they still remained memorable each time.

JOHN LAWSON   I first saw Celtic in 1940. I was 11. It was a dream come true. I'd been brought up in a football family; so, as a boy, I'd listened to tales that my father told me about the great Patsy Gallagher. He would give me descriptions of the goal Gallagher scored against Dundee in the Cup final, when he did a somersault into the back of the net with the ball . . .

SANDRA LEWSEY   My first memory was being lifted over, as they called it, by my dad, reluctantly taking me to the football after me going on and on about it. I went as regularly as my dad would take me. I moaned and moaned and followed him out the house when he was going to games on a Saturday. Sometimes he relented and took me, other times he was devious and left me with my mother.

EUGENE MacBRIDE   You were dyed in the wool Celtic. I remember one time serving on the altar at Holy Cross. Celtic were up the road playing Rangers in a Glasgow Cup or a Charity Cup tie, and someone would play a joke; 'Celtic won, Celtic won!' You'd go, 'What?' 'Celtic won, Rangers three . . .' And the bottom would just fall out of you. But when Celtic had a good win – I can remember my father, at one time, hanging out the window shouting down to me down on the back green that Celtic had done it – and, I tell you, you just took off. My father was an easy-osey man who had bursts of anger; I only saw him manifest joy when he was cheering a Celtic goal. He'd get up on his feet, if we were in the stand, on his feet. It was his life.

BILL McARTHUR   I was born and bred in Govan; my family was nicknamed the Bluenose McArthurs – bluenoses because at one time we used to paint our noses blue – and I continued the family tradition. Back in the mid-'30s my father took me as a child; I can remember seeing Alan Morton running down the wing. When I got a bit older, it took over; we played Boys' Brigade football in the morning, came home for lunch, went to Ibrox in the afternoon.

JOHNNY PATON   As a boy I attended St Mary's Church in Abercromby Street, in the East End of Glasgow, what you call the Calton, where Celtic originated. My grandfather had a little confectionery shop right opposite the church; he had the number 2 season ticket and he was always very, very upset that he didn't have the number 1. I went to all the Celtic matches way back in the '30s and sat on his knee on the number 2 seat, directly behind the old directors' box. By the time I came to play for Celtic, my mind had been quite glamorised by the players I saw – like Jimmy McGrory, whom I remember seeing break the world goal-scoring record, three goals in four minutes, so they say.

ALAN GALLOWAY   My first memories are of going with my father. He used to take us to the Rangers End; I had the worm's-eye view, down at the front with all the kids, standing on the terraces. When I was a bit older I went with my uncle, who was a season-ticket holder; I remember being taken down to Merkland Street in Partick and standing outside the pub while my uncle Robert went in with all his pals, then going on the underground to the Copland Road. Nine or ten years old, but you felt the excitement.

JOHN WATSON   As a boy you felt every result. If we lost my mum would be in saying, 'It's only a game.' But I'd be in the bedroom, just lying there, light out, not going out.

COLIN GLASS   My father died when I was ten; my mother was in her early fifties and very much against the idea of her only son going into Glasgow where so many nasty things apparently happened. She was very set against it – I remember badgering the life out of her to let me go and see this Cup tie between Rangers and Hibs. At first she let me, then she took me off the train because she changed her mind. It caused major bad feeling and a deterioration of school performance for many, many months – basically I rebelled in quite a major way.

JOHN LARKIN   When I first went to Parkhead I wasn't 'allowed' but I couldn't stay away so I told my mum and dad I was going to the pictures. They said, 'What picture are you going to see?' I told them the name of one; I'd already seen it. I had it all worked out in advance, so that when they asked what the picture was like I could tell them. So everything was okay – except a guy just along from me in the ground got lifted that night, and there was a picture of that bit of the crowd right in the paper!

ALEX MacDONALD My background was very much a Rangers one. I came from Tradeston and I was actually born in Scotland Street, down towards Ibrox. Around there everything was orientated towards Rangers; we stayed off school to go down and watch them training and stuff like that. I used to stand on the terraces at the Celtic End and give them V-signs. On Sundays we'd sneak into Ibrox and play two-a-side the full length of the park! Even when I was up playing at St Johnstone, if there were any European games we used to go down to Ibrox – standing behind the dug-out, you know.

JOHN McPHAIL I was at St Mungo's Academy in the East End – a real Celtic hotbed. We played in the final of the Scottish Schools' Shield; we beat Falkirk High and Bobby Brown, the great Rangers goalkeeper, was their captain. They had wiped the floor with us 4–1 and 4–0 in the League; but when we met them in the final, we wore Celtic jerseys. Wearing the hoops made a difference, no question; we hammered them 3–1.

ALEC WILLOUGHBY I came from a Rangers family, very much a Rangers family – father, brothers, uncles, aunts, cousins, nephews. All bluenoses. As a laddie growing up in the early '50s, I would travel on the Townhead and Springburn Rangers bus; it was the biggest club in the Supporters' Association, with two or three buses leaving for Ibrox every Saturday. When I captained the Scottish Schoolboys there were 32 clubs trying to sign me; being a Glasgow boy and a Protestant, there was only one club I wanted to play for.

ALEX BELL I came down to London when I was 19 or 20; I joined a band – The Lovers – and we were playing with Lulu. I was the guitarist. We had all been working in Glasgow; I had been an apprentice electrician; we made a record, the record got into the Top 10, we packed our bags and left. The record was

'Shout', of course. The band was mixed; we had two steaming-hot Celtic supporters and two Rangers supporters. I used to share a flat with the bass-player; he and I used to travel back home together for the Cup final. We'd split up to watch the game and meet up after. We used to phone from Poland, Germany, anywhere in the world if there was a Celtic-Rangers game on; the first thing we did was reach for the phone and find out the result.

EDDIE McGRAW We came to Auchenairn in 1949 and since then I haven't missed a great deal of Celtic games. Before that it was an odd home game. Mary and I, we were winching quite young, too – so if I went anywhere, maybe to an away game, I had to be home for whatever dancing we were going to. So winching became a wee bit more important than Celtic for maybe a couple of weeks. But then you went back to your first love – see?

STUART DANIELS Even the day I got married I went to see Rangers – 24th April, 1971. I was through at Kilmarnock that day, without my wife, and I came back at night. I've heard various individuals say that they went to church and had a wireless and that – but it doesn't wash with me. I was there that day at Rugby Park. Well, there's only one Rangers – there's plenty wives.

GEORGE MOORE I got married in 1967; it was the year Celtic went on to win the European Cup. We got married in the morning – at that time you had the wedding breakfast, and the reception was normally at night. So she says, 'What will we do in the afternoon?' She's looking at all these theatres and whatnot – 'George, the ballet's on.' I just got a cab – myself and the wife and the best man – to Celtic Park. When we came out the match we couldn't find a taxi to get back so we were the last into the reception. Everybody was waiting on us!

HUGH TONER There was a chap very 'happy' after a game down at Sunderland and people were asking him where he stayed. Let's say it was in the Maryhill Road area. So they drove him home up to Glasgow, took him up to the door. And his mother says, 'What are you doing here? You're supposed to be on your honeymoon!' It turned out he'd been down on the coast and had gone over to Roker Park for the game. The other fans thought they were doing him a good turn taking him home. Meanwhile his new wife's sitting in front of the telly in Whitley Bay!

MARGARET DEVLIN   I always went to the stand at Celtic Park. At that time we used to always go in the same turnstile; and we're going through one night and the chap at the other side said, 'You again? You must give this club all your wages!' And he looked around and said, 'Jump over!' Now he had only seen me from the chest up – he didn't know that I was about eight months pregnant with Mary-Jo, my eldest. I said, 'Oh no, no, no . . .' 'Jump over,' he said, 'you've given them enough money.' So there I am clambering over these turnstiles at eight months pregnant.

HUGH FERRIE   I've got a friend who was a doctor; I won't mention his name. He was called out to a house in Lanarkshire. A child had been very badly burned – I think it was boiling water over him or something – and the child had to be rushed to hospital. The husband was putting his coat on. The doctor said, 'This child's very ill. Have to get him to hospital.' 'I canny take him,' the man says. 'Celtic are playing Leeds United tonight.' And he went out.

SANDY STRANG   My grandfather was a watchmaker in Pollokshaws – a quiet, introspective man, very much a community man.
  It was a five-and-a-half day week; well, six-and-a-half day, since Sunday was spent doing the repairs. But Saturday afternoon was religiously kept – the scarf came out the drawer and we all went along to Ibrox, where he had a season ticket.

BRIAN CRAIG   In financial terms being a supporter has cost me quite a lot. I've lost three jobs through it; when I ran out of holidays and still travelled abroad to a game the scenario was usually that when I came home again I'd have no job to go to. But quite a few's done that, so . . .

JOHN LAWSON I'm retired now. I've been watching for 55 years. I've enjoyed every minute of it and I'm still in desperation every Saturday afternoon to get away.

EDDIE McGRAW My reaction will always be the same: I'll be supporting Celtic as long as I can, as long as I'm fit to go. Celtic's the only hobby Mary and I've got now, apart from the swimming; we're getting too old for the dancing. I buy Celtic songs and I've all the Celtic tapes in there – I've 17 Celtic tapes and I'll be leaving them for someone else to see. Not for a wee while yet, right enough!

GEORGE MacLEOD I'm working on her to let me be scattered over Ibrox when the time comes. She's not so keen, right enough.

DAVID PALMER Bigotry aside, the people of Glasgow have an incredible passion for football. It's not just the ones who turn up for the match, though I believe that if there was a ground that still had a capacity of 90,000, they could still fill it for an Old Firm match and I don't really think there's any match in Britain that you could say that about. The result does mean so much to so many people – everybody always remembers the result of the last one, and if Rangers have lost the last one there's this kind of sense of holding your breath until we meet again, when revenge may, or may not, be sweet.

Chapter Two

DOMESTIC TIFFS 1945–1955

The 1940s and '50s were good times for Rangers and mixed times for Celtic. Rangers enjoyed a settled period of strength over the whole decade; Celtic fans had to wait five or six years after the end of the war for their street-parties to begin.

Post-war football in Glasgow began in earnest in 1945 with a challenge match between the great Rangers team dubbed the 'Iron Curtain' and the men from behind the Curtain itself, Moscow Dynamo. To war-dulled eyes the visitors, who handed over bouquets of flowers before kick-off, seemed exotic. The stature of the fixture convinced Glaswegians that the war – with its phoney war football fixtures – was at an end and that they were back in the big league. The match caused a huge stir of excitement.

. . . everybody was looking for heroes, I suppose . . .

JACK JARDINE It's actually the first match I remember, the Moscow Dynamo match. For obvious reasons – there was some build-up, everybody talking about them. They were the team that had been running riot and smashing Chelsea 10–1 and whatnot. It was built up as a great occasion. The end of the war – everybody was looking for heroes, I suppose. For the working class just after the war, football was it. I mean, they'd been starved, during the war, of everything. Football was when they could let themselves go, you know; either that or it was at *The*

Jolson Story! There was no telly or nothing, so I suppose maybe we had nothing else – it was our life.

JIM COOKE   It was one of the first all-ticket games and up to two days before the game we were still grilling round for tickets. It was a midweek game, a Wednesday I think, and of course we should have been working. But even if you worked there were ways of getting to the games if you were keen. There were a lot of grannies passed away that week.

JOCK SHAW   It was a very special atmosphere; a complete sell-out; you couldn't get a ticket for love nor money. It was one of those games that was just exciting from the start to the finish. But they were a lot of fly men, they Russians. At one point Torry Gillick actually counted the Russian team and they were fielding 12 men. In those days we didn't have substitutes here; this was the first I'd heard of substitutes, and they sneaked one on without notifying the referee. Torry said to me, 'Listen – that man was supposed to go off and they've brought on another player.' I had to go to the referee; he sent him off.

The Victory Cup Old Firm match, held in June 1946, is nicely emblematic of the relative states of the Old Firm teams at the end of the war. Rangers had maintained a strong team throughout the war years, and inflicted several heavy defeats on Celtic while amassing a long run of war-time Championships. Celtic, on the other hand, had struggled badly, partly as a result of boardroom policy.

the referee was smelling of drink . . .

MATT LYNCH   The Victory Cup – I remember that. Celtic–Rangers. There was trouble; I think we were drawing and Rangers got their usual penalty kick; Willie Thornton stumbled and a penalty kick was given by a referee that they said was smelling of drink. The penalty kick was naturally hotly disputed and Jimmy Mallan, God rest him, was over trying to obliterate the penalty spot while the argument about whether it was or wasn't a penalty was going on. So the referee sent Jimmy off.

Then George Patterson had the ball and was arguing with him – naturally – and the referee says, 'The ball please.' And George reputedly said, 'Here you are – it's like yourself, full of wind.' So he was sent inside and all. So Rangers got their penalty and scored with it. We finished with two off, which left nine; seven, really, since we had two partly crippled; so it was a glorious victory for Rangers.

JOHNNY PATON   My legs still feel tired today.

JOHN McPHAIL   I had signed in June 1941; terrible times for Celtic. There were good players stationed all over the place at that time, whether with the Army or the RAF or whatever. But Celtic wouldn't play guest players. White was the chairman and he wouldn't invite guest players to come and play. So we were struggling away with whoever was coming up and the old ones that were left over; everyone else was in the army.

JOHNNY PATON   One day after training I was just out the bath and I was round at the number 11 peg; the number 11 peg is the one nearest the door. There was a knock at the door, which was most unusual because in those days the first-team dressing-room was holy ground. I opened the door and there was a man standing there in an ordinary soldier's uniform. I said, 'Can I help you?' He says, 'I'd like to see the manager.' I said, 'The manager's not here. Sometimes we don't see him much during the week. But the trainer's here.' I went over to the treatment room and Alec Dowdells was there, and I said, 'Alec, there's a soldier here wants to see somebody.' He said, 'What does he want?' I said, 'He wants to play for Celtic.' And Alec says, 'You must be joking'. I said, 'He's insisting he wants to see the manager.' And Alec says, 'Go and ask him what his name is.' I came back and I said to Alec, 'I've never heard of him. His name's Matt Busby.'

I presume he came back and was told about Celtic's policy of not playing guest players. They relied on a youth policy only. It was one of their downfalls. Busby went on to Hibs and he transformed Hibs – they won the League and the Cup while he was with them. Hibs' gain was Celtic's loss.

FRANK MOOTY   It was miserable watching them at that time; we seemed to have nobody at all. You'd Matt Busby dying to play for Celtic, and Bill Shankly, who went to Partick Thistle. I remember Matthews and Lawton playing for Morton or Airdrie. Hamilton Accies had guest players every day of the week – big Frank Swift the goalkeeper; Alex Baird, the internationalist; big McShane of Blackburn Rovers, the fellow whose son is on TV. We had nobody. Meanwhile the Rangers were that strong they had two teams; they had another team in the north-east and the Rangers second team could have beat the Celtic.

. . . just cheerio – and away he went to Man United . . .

JOHNNY PATON   Celtic were in a bit of a mess and I think the last hope they had of doing something about it went when Jimmy Delaney went to Manchester United in 1946. I always remember the day he went. Jimmy was having problems with Celtic – he felt he wasn't getting his just rewards. He came in that day and he says to Alec Dowdells, 'Give me my boots, Alec.' So Alec gave him the boots. 'Have you got a bit of paper?' says Delaney. 'A bit of brown paper.' Alec says, 'What do you want a bit of paper for?' Delaney says, 'A bit of brown paper.' And Alec got a bit of brown paper and he wrapped his boots in it. And then it was just cheerio – no carry on or anything – just cheerio – and away he went to Man United!

NEIL McDERMOTT   After Delaney, there was a phrase in common parlance at the time to describe the Celtic forward line – they called them 'The Five Sorrowful Mysteries'. It was one of the jokes; somebody seeing the Celtic manager standing at a butcher's shop: 'What are you doing here, Mr McGrory?' 'Oh, I'm getting a pound of sausages for John McPhail.' 'Well, you're getting a bargain.' John McPhail's a bad example, in fact – he was one of their better players.

EUGENE MacBRIDE   Things got so bad, I once went to Rangers! Some Catholic boys got so fed up they switched their allegiance. I can remember one summer's day in 1946 going to the League Cup at Ibrox with a boy called Lennon from Dixon Avenue and we watched Rangers beating Morton 1–0. But all I was anxious about was hearing the Celtic score over the tannoy – Celtic were playing Thirds that same day.

The Rangers team of the period immediately after the war – the Iron Curtain team – sticks firmly in the mind of those who saw it play. This is partly a matter of the team's personnel (in the memory at least the team rarely varied in its line-up) and partly a matter of style. The team played according to a tactical plan that many fans remember as ultra-defensive; though perhaps the myth of the Iron Curtain has outrun the reality of a team which also possessed creative midfield players such as the numerate Torry Gillick. Either way, fans still faithfully recite, in one version or another, the Rangers eleven that turned out after the war.

JIMMY BROWN   It went something like this: Brown, Young and Shaw; McColl, Woodburn and Cox; Waddell, Gillick, Thornton, Duncanson and Caskie. It rarely changed.

IAN McCOLL   I came into the side as the youngest player in 1945. The Iron Curtain tag was a piece of journalistic licence. We never set out to be defensive; it just happened that we played very well together and we didn't lose many goals. We were able to build up an unusual understanding; the team went unchanged for years. We won the Cup in 1948, 1949 and 1950; the same defence played in all three finals. The forward line only changed in about three places over those years – I mean three different people. So in the three Cup finals there were maybe only 15 players used – 14 or 15 players in three years.

Rangers were the only team that came out for the second half wearing a new strip . . .

BILL LAMOND   From the terraces, they always seemed to be based on defence. It seemed telepathic at times. Their ploy was to stop the other team scoring, then go down the pitch, get

31

a corner kick and Thornton would put it in the back of the net and that was the job done – the midfield could go back home.

They also did things differently from everybody else; they were the only team I knew who came out for the second half with a new strip. I think it was all part of a ploy to intimidate the other team, to tell them how poor they all were, that Rangers could afford to wash two strips at the weekend.

FRANK MOOTY They broke our hearts, the Iron Curtain team. This was all when I was just a boy and the Rangers were hammering us. Willie Waddell was the main one; he always had a new lace in his left boot. No new lace in his right boot; but a new white football lace in his left boot.

JACK JARDINE Their whole game was a matter of soaking it up and getting it out to Waddell. When it started to look as if the ball was going out towards Waddell the roar started, and it'd build up into a crescendo until Waddell got that ball. He was everybody's hero. He was like a hare and he used to get on to that ball and everybody was all shouting, just a mass of roaring. What I remember was the excitement; I can't explain the difference, except to say that you were more engrossed.

You actually sort of qualified as a spectator when I was wee; you started by going to see the Juniors, the Wee Rangers – you were allowed to go to that yourself and you sort of graduated from them to the reserves and then to the Saturday. Saturday was the big day – the Juniors would maybe play midweek, but the big thing was the Saturday. When you were young the matinee was a great thing but the real big thing was getting to the football; with all the older ones, the shouting, the patter; and you used to get groups and they all had their carry-out beside them, their cans and their whisky.

ALEX BELL At Ibrox, where the players came out of the tunnel, as they came out onto the pitch there used to be a bit that was cordonned off for the band that used to play before the game and at half-time. It was a little fenced-off enclosure and I used to sit just down by there with my legs over the wall, by the cinder track. This was about '48, '49; my father would come down to the games with his old cronies from the army, because he had been in the same regiment as Willie Thornton. All I seem to remember is Rangers winning a lot; because we won every year the memories aren't very specific; they're little snatches. I remember seeing Willie Woodburn getting ordered off once playing against a right-back who played for Clyde called Albert Murphy. I remember the atmosphere being pretty electric so much so that my dad wouldn't take me to the Celtic games, though I saw the Hibs, the Hearts. One of my memories is of him coming down from where he was standing and dragging me off the wall and taking me up to the back with him when things were about to turn nasty.

EUGENE MacBRIDE We were always interested in a Rangers defeat – because it happened so rarely, I suppose. As a boy I could not comprehend how the hell Rangers ever got beat. Rangers went to Germany in 1945 and the British Army on the Rhine hammered them 6–1. I could not comprehend that! And then Clyde one night beat them 4–3. I remember saying to my father, 'Why is it that Rangers are so good?' This is walking across Glasgow to Parkhead from Pollokshaws Road, way across Polmadie, Glasgow Green, up to Brigton Cross – 'Why are Rangers so good?' And I remember my father saying, 'They're not all that good. They're just better than the others.'

Rangers' Iron Curtain side had been given birth to and nourished by Bill Struth, whose period as Rangers manager spanned a remarkable 34 years before he handed over to Scot Symon in June 1954. Struth was very much a man of his period, and belonged to the tradition of Rangers' managers before Souness – straight, intimidating, businesslike, an upkeeper of presbyterian values.

JOCK SHAW Mr Struth was the manager – we called him the Boss, he was never anything else. He was a very, very strict man, and of course it all just came right down from him.

IAN McCOLL   Bill Struth had not been a player, he had been a trainer. The training was nonetheless very primitive; it was unsupervised. But one of Struth's skills was his choice of players – he chose players who would get on with their training; so unsupervised training was possible. I was very fit when I was there – we were certainly fitter than everyone else.

Struth never appeared on the touch-line. Scot Symon was the first Rangers manager to do that. I had an argument with him about it; I was actually on the ball, seeing the game one way, he saw it another and his shouting made me lose concentration. We had some words about it afterwards. But Struth would never come near the touch-line. Struth was conservative; he was the one who prevented Rangers from entering the European Cup; he didn't think it was the thing for Rangers. So Hibs were invited, later in the 1950s. Though we did play friendlies against European teams.

JOCK SHAW   We played a lot of European friendlies, but it wasn't a league like today. We played Benfica in Portugal; we played in Sweden, Switzerland, Belgium, Germany. Those were the highlights of the season.

JOHNNY BONNAR   At that time there wasn't much travel. Celtic did go to Rome to play Lazio in 1950; what an experience. We were rigged out in these beautiful blazers. It took five days to go to Rome. We travelled by train – unbelievable, in this day and age. We left Glasgow in the morning and we stayed the night in the Imperial Hotel in London; the following morning we went over by train and ferry to Brussels and stayed the night there; the following morning we went down through France and stayed in Lucerne; the following night we stayed in Milan. We arrived in Rome the following day; the same thing on the way back. For one game – a no-scoring draw!

Celtic used to go to Ireland every year – we played charity games over there. The Irish would always clap you onto the field; you'd come out the dressing-room and they'd be lined up in the tunnel, clapping you on. But once they got you on the field they'd try to kick you off it! There were two brothers in particular called Noonan – one played right-back for Cork City – he'd kick anything that moved. But it was all politeness till you got on the park; it was like rugby. Brutal.

On the other side of the city from Struth's Ibrox the man in charge was Jimmy McGrory. McGrory had been a player whose exploits were the stuff of legend; but his derring-do as a player did not ensure that he would become a capable manager of Celtic. And even if he had had it in him to do so, it was never clear whether the Celtic chairman of the day would have granted him the freedom to do it to the best of his abilities.

JOHN McPHAIL McGrory had come as manager in 1945. Jimmy was just a great player, to me; we were delighted to meet the old chap, and his name was history itself. I'm afraid things didn't work out.

MATT LYNCH I had actually played with McGrory. When Celtic won the Scottish Cup in 1937 we went on a tour of the Highlands. I can remember they treated the Scottish Cup with contempt; it was wrapped up and thrown in a luggage rack, and we stopped at each village and polished it up to show it off. I remember I played a game up there; I think it was in Nairn. McGrory was centre-forward and I crossed three balls from the wing – just the normal, poor sort of crosses. And they finished up in the net and McGrory ran over as if they were perfect crosses. God, did he make me feel good.

As a manager he wouldn't have tried anything new, though; he followed in the footsteps of the men before him. There were no tactics, just a few instructions you were supposed to keep to. A good example of how players would behave at that time happened one time at Tynecastle. There was a big fellow who had played schools football with me, Dykes you called him, a centre-half. We were playing this game and Andy Anderson the Scottish international was right-back and Dykes was centre-half. Some of our boys were interchanging – something they'd worked out amongst themselves – but it meant that for a bit the three of them were over, opposed to Anderson and his right-half. And Anderson shouted, 'Dykes – get over and cover.' And

Dykes said, 'I was telt to stay here and I'm staying here!' This was right in front of the goal you know! You got instructions; you stuck to them; that's the extreme case, but there was still plenty of that sort of spirit when McGrory came.

He was too fine a gentleman to be a successful manager – I think you need to be a bit of a you-know-what. Jock Stein, or so I heard, really went to town after a poor start, so much so that on some Saturdays Bob Kelly used to leave the dressing-room. McGrory never raged into you; which meant that unfortunately you felt as though you were never playing a bad game.

In the late '40s and early '50s the Scottish League had a number of teams challenging for honours. Among them were not only the clubs that a modern spectator would expect – the Aberdeens and the Motherwells of this world – but also a number of clubs whose power in the land has proved even more transitory – Morton, Clyde, East Fife. In the Eden-like world of pre-motorway Scotland teams such as these and a host of others (Cowdenbeath, Arbroath, Queen of the South) could attract and hold a big and loyal local support. Often made up of people who had to work until 12 o'clock on a Saturday, these crowds did not have the opportunity to travel to Glasgow, as many of their descendants have chosen to do in preference to supporting their local team. And although Old Firm supporters take pride in the drawing of support from areas outwith Glasgow, it is indisputable that the League the Old Firm teams have dominated in the last 20 or 30 years has been the weaker for it.

The major rivalry of this period was not an Old Firm affair; mainly because Celtic had a poor team which did not win the post-war Championship until their 1953–54 Double season. Between the end of the war and then, the champions were either the Iron Curtain Rangers side or the Hibernian side, whose forward line became known as the Famous Five and whose flamboyant and exciting play gave birth to far more enduring childhood fantasies than the novels of Enid Blyton.

BILL LAMOND   Rangers victories were founded on defence, whereas the Hibs team was an attacking team. Rangers were – if you don't let them in, you've a good chance of winning; up front Hibs had one of those line-ups that everyone remembers – Smith, Johnstone, Reilly, Turnbull, Ormond. The games at Easter Road and Ibrox were regularly full houses with a tremendous atmosphere – the Celtic–Rangers of that time – Rangers–Hibs became the biggest game. To see the fascinating difference in styles . . . the flair that Hibs had, but they never had the best of defences and Rangers, with Willie Waddell and Willie Thornton, could exploit that. But at times the Famous Five were more than a match for the Iron Curtain.

. . . Four penalties in one game . . .

JOHNNY BONNAR The Famous Five were brilliant. I remember playing at Easter Road in a League game. We'd a left-back at that time who was inclined to lose his head at times – Jimmy Mallan, his name was. Gordon Smith came down the wing and Jimmy scythed him – penalty kick. Eddie Turnbull, who was one of the hardest kickers of a ball I've ever come across, he took it; as he ran up I says, 'I'll dive to my right'; he hit it to my left. Not long after they got another penalty; as he ran up I says, 'This time I'll dive to the left.' He hit it into the right. Second half they got another penalty. This time I says, 'He'll change it again,' so I dived to the left; he hit it to the right. Near the end of the game they got another penalty. I guessed right! Well, I got my hands to it. It nearly tore my hands off going into the net. Four penalties in the one game.

IAN McCOLL Most of the League Championships were between Rangers and Hibs. To tell you the truth I can't remember many of the Championship campaigns individually. One of the most memorable didn't feature Hibs, however. There was one season, 1948–49, when Dundee lost 4–1 on the last day to Falkirk and we won the title. Jerry Dawson was playing for Falkirk at that time and saved a penalty. Dundee were a good side, good players, a big support – I think Billy Steel was playing for them then. People would say they lost the League on the last day, but that's not the way it works. You might as well say they lost it on the first day or on any other day they lost.

GEORGE MacLEOD In 1950 they played Hibs, a head to head for the title; I remember it only because of what was happening in my family. I had a brother who had been taken ill with some kind of lung problem and he was being kept in isolation. My mother was visiting him and I suppose my father was under orders to look after the wean kind of thing. As the morning went by my father was getting more and more restless – reading the paper, putting it down, reading the paper again. And finally, about 12 o'clock, he just stood up and said something like 'I'm not missing it.' He made me put my coat on and he took me down to this game at Ibrox. Lifted over, down to the front. Rangers just needed to draw to win the League; a draw and Hibs would be finished. And all I remember is Hibs on the attack for nearly the whole game but never really seeming to get anywhere, and Rangers in the royal blue kind of rugby shirts and the long shorts, these big men standing firm, holding the line. And it finished 0–0. I was only seven or eight, still at the stage you miss most of what's happening. And my brother got better –he was out that summer. We all went down to Dunoon or somewhere for a fortnight. Doctor's orders. Unheard of.

JIM COOKE Rangers were playing Aberdeen in the Cup final sometime in the early '50s, I suppose, and my wife and I had been invited out, and of course when you were invited out you'd to go dressed. So I had on a white shirt, a red tie, a heavy coat, my gloves, all the rest of it. Standing on the huge, open terracings at Hampden; and of course the heavens opened. First the gloves got thrown away, then the shirt was all red off the tie, so the tie went . . . When we came back my wife gave me a piece of her mind. We won the Cup right enough; so it was probably worth the earful.

GEORGE MacLEOD I remember when I was a bit older being taken down to Dumfries one year to see them win the League – on goal average, as they called it then. They needed a draw and Waddell equalised, quite late on, I think.

IAN McCOLL In that game against Queen of the South George Young was giving the referee a bit of chat; it looked like backchat, an argument because Queen of the South had a free-kick and they were pushing men forward. As it turned out the referee was a Rangers supporter and – so they said afterwards – he was telling George that if the goal went in for Queen of the South then he would disallow it!

. . . Celtic were hardly at the races then . . .

JACK JARDINE   Celtic were hardly at the races then. Of course it was always a big game, the Rangers–Celtic; but the Rangers–Hibs games were the real big games at that time. I always remember the semi-finals of the Cup – it must have been in about 1947, maybe 1948. Morton were playing Celtic and Rangers were playing Hibs. I think it's said that there were 140-odd thousand there for the Rangers–Hibs game – unbelievable numbers. I remember going up Greenfield Street in Govan, where I lived; and there were quite a few Irish people staying up the top of Greenfield Street. And I remember them shouting, hanging out the windows, like: 'It's going to be Celtic and Hibs, it's going to be the battle of the greens in the final!' – it was so good when it turned out that Morton beat Celtic and Rangers beat Hibs. So it was an all-blue final instead of an all-green final.

EUGENE MacBRIDE   I remember the time of the 1948 Scottish Cup semi-final. Celtic had gone to Ibrox to play Morton, and Morton were a very good side. We lived in Pollokshaws Road at that time; there was no radio, we didn't have a radio – and I was waiting around the close-mouth for the result to come from Ibrox – and it had gone to extra-time so it was getting later and later, darker and darker – and then the score came along, passed along the road by word of mouth; 1–0 for Morton. That was a kick in the teeth.

We actually bought a radio soon after that; sometime in 1948. We bought a radio on the never never and I had to go into town every Saturday and pay sixpence or whatever. Peter Thomson was the commentator's name – he was supposed to be an out-and-out Rangers supporter. But he was a magnificent commentator – he put Raymond Glendenning to shame.

Before that, one of the most delicious sensations was to go into the newspaper shop when the pink *Times* was there, the green *Citizen* was there, some of the other papers – Glasgow was glutted with newspapers – and you'd glance at the results and you'd see that Celtic had won at Brockville. You were in ecstasies. That Saturday evening newspaper – I used to read them all, every one I could lay my hands on – I'd read them from cover to cover. I read all the senior games, I read all the junior games, I read all the comment – I was a total expert at the age of ten.

And then there were the Sunday papers; you'd get the *Sunday Post*, the *Sunday Mail* – we didn't go for anything else. But again you would devour. In fact that was where I first discovered that there was such a thing as literary style – I suddenly realised that all these football writers had the same style. 'Rex' in the *Sunday Mail* or Jack Harkness in the *Sunday Post*. Of course as I got older I couldn't take it any more; I realised I was reading a lot of pap.

ALEX BELL Nowadays they're saturated with television; my boy is football daft. At that time the only way of seeing pictures was in the cinema; I remember seeing Scotland playing England at Wembley on British Movietone News or Pathé Pictorial. It was always wonderful – very, very short and a long shot but lovely, up there on a big screen. But I don't remember seeing Rangers on television. We were still in the era when it was best to go and see the matches; there was no substitute for going.

Meanwhile Celtic's post-war blues were deep and getting deeper. Not only did they have to endure the Green–Blue rivalry failing to include their particular shade of green; they also had a brush with relegation. There is some dispute still about how close they really were to the drop; but even if the ring didn't go round the finger it was certainly more than a flirtation. These days football's administrators have created a cushioned landing for teams dropping through the trap-door in both Scotland and England; nowadays you can go down and still be in the 'First' Division. In 1947–48 Celtic were facing what was, without any such obfuscation, the 'Second' Division when they played a crucial match with Dundee at Dens Park.

JOHN McPHAIL   The strange thing was that we could have won the Scottish Cup that year. In the semi-final, a couple of players missed open goals before the final whistle; it went to extra-time and Morton beat us. We could have been through to the final against Rangers. But everything just started to fall apart and we kept losing game after game. When we went to Dens, with four or five games to go, we knew if we won that one the rest could cut themselves to pieces.

I think I was made captain that day for that game at Dundee. We scored first – I'm sure we scored first – and then we scored another two which were knocked off; a piece of nonsense. We had great debates and discussions about the refereeing that day. At half-time we should have had a two- or three-goal lead. Dundee hammered us after the interval; they had two into the net within five or ten minutes. So it was all gloom and doom and misery. But we'd bought a wee fellow from Middlesbrough called Jock Weir; Jock scored an equaliser and managed another with just a few minutes to go. And just on the final whistle I hit the ball, the goalkeeper palmed down and wee Jock was in on the line to shoot it past him to make sure. So wee Jock had got his hat-trick and we were safe.

MATT LYNCH   That day through at Dundee, saved by the skin of our teeth – we felt like we'd got away with something that day. We were determined that that would never happen again.

Celtic stayed up, therefore, but in the following seasons they had little in the way of success. The support's spirits were raised by the arrival of a Northern Irishman called Charles Patrick Tully. The cheeky, gallus Tully was a character – just what a crowd watching a characterless team needed.

JOHNNY PATON   I remember going over to Belfast with Celtic to play in the five-a-sides; we had a very good five-a-side team and we played Belfast Celtic in the final. They had a youngster on the left side who was brilliant; a bag of tricks, he was; and it was Charlie Tully. They made him inside-left; I was on the left wing; Tully and Paton played on the left for three seasons.

He was a bit of a character; a lot of tricks with the ball and so on. He wasn't the originator of nutmegging; but he would put his own touch on it by running the ball through a player's legs, running round him, giving the player a chance to recover and then doing it to him again; and I'd never seen a player do that.

Charlie was so cheeky with what he did – they talk about tactics at throw-ins and all that carry on. Charlie would take a throw-in quick, shout 'there!', confuse the bloke, who'd turn his back and Charlie would throw the ball against his back, take the rebound and be round the back before the bloke had realised what happened.

I've never known a player anywhere – in Scotland, England, at Celtic, Arsenal – who developed such a charismatic relationship with the supporters. I remember one incident – it was in one of our very few victories over Rangers. When we got 2–0 up Charlie had a spell when he just dazzled. That's the only way I can describe it. I think it was a throw-back to some of the old stories of Tommy McInally and so on. He got the ball in midfield; he suddenly rushed at the Rangers defence and he stopped; and they all stopped; and Charlie stood on the ball; and he half-sat on it. He displayed it all in one night. Just like Baxter at Wembley in 1967 he simply mesmerised the opposition. That's when the charisma started with the Celtic Supporters' Club. Up to that point Charlie had been noticed but not all that much. But from that moment the supporters treated him as a messiah.

. . . when Tully's name was announced on the tannoy, you never knew who was playing outside-left because of the roar that went up . . .

EUGENE MacBRIDE   What I can remember was the 1940s when you'd get rolling waves of applause. You've no idea what it was like at Celtic Park to be standing there – and the ballboys coming out of the tunnel – and there's Bobby Hogg leading the team – and there's Willie Miller in the beautiful yellow jersey looking the part absolutely and all these athletic young men coming out in green and white. That was the most fantastic sensation.

And when Tully's name was announced on the tannoy you never knew who was playing outside-left because of the roar that went up. The crowd knew they were going to be entertained.

JOHNNY BONNAR   He was a brilliant dribbler; he could do tricks with the ball. He would sway his body about and leave everybody standing; he'd another trick – he'd use his hands to point to the outside-left and he'd point; and all the defenders would drift out towards the outside-left and of course he'd come back inside. We'd a player called Johnny Paton – great player. He could run like a hare; very fast. Charlie would get the ball at the centre of the field and stop it dead; and he would point to Johnny. The right-back and the right-half would step over to cover Johnny; Charlie would step in and put the ball to the other side of the field. He did it time and time again; they fell for it time and time again.

FRANK MOOTY   Everybody loved Tully because Tully came in 1948 when Celtic were really down and out. The Celtic love an idol – they love the Jimmy Johnstones, the Dixie Deanses; they seem to have to get the spotlight on one man. Well, Tully was our man at that time. All the jokes were about Tully, all the patter was about Tully. He would maybe play rubbish half the time but everybody forgot that; he would come out with something which people would remember, like the two corner kicks at Falkirk.

JOHN LAWSON   I was at Falkirk that day, standing beside the goal next to the railway station. Charlie put the ball down for the corner, took it, put it straight into the net. The referee blew, made him take it again. He put the ball down, took it again, did it again.

JOHN McPHAIL   There was one game I remember when Charlie Tully and Sammy Cox had a bit of a furore; about 1949 or 1950. Sammy had a bit of a go at Charlie and should have been booked or sent off. But then again Charlie was an actor; he made the most of it, you know. The two of them were great buddies, of course. They ended up drunk together that night. The crowd going berserk, Celtic and Rangers fans at each other's throats all over the city and they're out on the razzle!

JOHNNY PATON   This will give you an idea of his popularity; I was Players' Union rep at one stage, and I remember Charlie coming up to me and saying that a company wanted his photo to make jigsaws and what should he do? I said, 'Give them it – this only lasts a short time.' So you could say that that was the beginning of commercialism.

JOHNNY BONNAR   I do remember Charlie coming to the ground one day and finding a wee man selling postcards with pictures of him; he went mad! Yes, Tully was king, but you had a lot of other players too. Bobby Collins was a very powerful player. And then there was Bobby Evans.

. . . he used to read comics in the dressing-room . . .

JOHNNY PATON   Bobby Evans was a strange lad – he was almost a schoolboy – he used to come in and read comics in the dressing-room. The *Beano* or the *Dandy* or whatever it was. And he had this remarkable ability; you'd turn round to talk to him and he'd be asleep! Maybe at half-time when the manager was giving the team talk. He had a marvellous ability to relax. He'd hop on the massage table at half-time saying, 'Oh-oh, I'm a bit tight up here,' and he'd be sound asleep!

The first five years of the 1950s were much more successful for Celtic. They took the Scottish Cup in 1951 and, with a journeyman centre-half called Jock Stein in their team, achieved the domestic Double in 1953–54. Added to these were a couple of one-off pots; the St Mungo Cup, played for to celebrate the Festival of Britain; and the Coronation Cup, which marked the elevation of Princess Elizabeth in 1953.

HUGH TONER In '51 it was really my first Cup final; you had a wee fear – could they do it? It had been heartbreaking before; we had had some great teams – some adventurous teams – but they always seemed to fall at the final hurdle. I remember going to Hampden that day for the Cup final – full of confidence on the outside, but inside . . .

JOHN McPHAIL I had a very bad injury, a groin injury. What happened then couldn't happen now. They were resting me for the League games and bringing me back for the Cup, because I could only last 15 minutes even when they brought me back. So everything that had to be done had to be done in 15 minutes.

Against Motherwell in the final I'm looking up and there's a clock; Hampden was the only place with a clock. I made a couple of chances for Jock and wee Bobby Collins which they missed. And I'm looking at this clock again. Thirteen minutes; and I know, psychologically, I've got two or three minutes left. Joe Bailey cleared this ball. I beat Andy Paton in the air first then I think I stepped between the two full-backs. The goalkeeper came out and I think I tried to clip it over his head. It went low; I wasn't pretending that I hadn't made a mistake. I remember running round the back of the net and I've never showed emotion like it in my life. You could see the crowds on the terracing going berserk.

The ovation when we won that game was fantastic. Sir Bob Kelly had become chairman by then, and I remember after the game we were getting off the bus and he turned to me and said, 'John, you've given me my first night's sleep for months.'

JOHNNY BONNAR In 1953 we had the Coronation Cup. On the Saturday we played Queen's Park in the final of the Charity Cup; Neilly Mochan got transferred in time for that game. On the Monday night we played Arsenal at Hampden; we won 1–0. On the Saturday we played Manchester United at Hampden in the semi-final and won 3–2, I think. The following Wednesday we played Hibs in the final; we beat them 2–0 and Mochan scored again. So Neilly got two medals before he'd played a game at Parkhead.

JOHN McPHAIL   Stein came in '52 to coach the reserves, supposed to be. To bring them on a bit you know. He was a damn good player. I played against him when he was at Albion Rovers and he was a hatchet man. When I heard that he was coming back, I was delighted; I said that's what we need here, a big hard man. He could also knee a ball. It became an art with him. The crowd loved it and he did it expertly. Instead of getting a foot back, he would just produce a knee and it would skite away about 40 yards, down the field.

JOHNNY BONNAR   We conceded just seven goals at Parkhead in the '53 Double season. The only game I remember was the last one; we beat Hibs 3–1 at Easter Road. In the Cup we beat Aberdeen 2–1; a good game. Huge crowd. We scored – in the second half – and Aberdeen came straight back up and equalised. Then with a few minutes left Sean Fallon scored; Willie Fernie was playing and Willie was a great dribbler of the ball; he beat the defence and cut the ball back; Sean had only to tap it in.

DAVID POTTER   That final was my first clear memory of anything to do with football: I got a shouting at from my father during the radio commentary of the Scottish Cup final between Celtic and Aberdeen for sliding along the floor to impersonate my hero, the Celtic goalkeeper Johnny Bonnar. I do remember my father going bananas at the final whistle.

JOHNNY BONNAR   The following year we got to the final again; we lost to Clyde in a replay. I gave away a goal in the first game – three minutes to go. We should have been four goals up but we were only one up and Archie Robertson took this corner kick. Now there was a high wind that day; you got that at Hampden, it was a bowl. I remember going for the ball, intending to clutch it by the bar. And the wind lifted the ball slightly; it was a new ball, you always played with a new ball, and funnily enough a new ball was affected by the wind; it rose above me and I just got my fingertips to it. If I had gone up with one hand I could have put it over the bar; I went up to catch it. At the last minute it took a deflection, a slight deflection; I got my fingertips to it but it went into the goal behind me. I was shattered.

DAVID POTTER The 1955 final I saw. It was on my auntie's TV; a small black-and-white job, but watched by loads of neighbours. My concentration faded in the second half and I went out to play football on the street, so I missed Clyde's horrific last-minute equaliser!

The immediate post-war era seems like a lost world now – the spread of powerful teams all around Scotland; the huge crowds packing in without the need for the exotic attractions of Europe; the rhythm of work, pub, game, soon to be lost with the end of Saturday working and the growing affluence of Britain in the '50s. What would also soon be lost was the sight of boys playing football on every street corner; it was perfectly understandable that no one really saw that with the disappearance of those endless games the power of Scotland as a force in world football would also disappear. Amongst the children playing in the 1940s and 1950s were the Denis Laws of this world; when will we see their likes again? The paradox was that the men who ran the clubs were not particularly enlightened in the way they brought boys on; yet the boys did come on.

JOHNNY PATON I couldn't wait to get home and play football, every night, seven nights a week. We used to play in St Mary's playground. I was only a youngster, probably only 11 or 12, but I was playing amongst men because there was a lot of unemployment in those days. They called them the cornerboys – they'd nothing else to do but to go round and play football and I used to go round and get in amongst that. Now they had four cement walls, and these guys thought nothing of battering you up against the wall. I think that's where the wall pass originated! You learned to hit the ball against the wall and run round them as fast as you could. It amuses me to hear world-class coaches and managers talking about trying to get players to play the wall pass as they get near the penalty area. We were doing it as kids naturally; you did it or else you got hurt.

JOHN McPHAIL   We thought the pace of the game was fast; but then again we were wearing these boots; we were like pit ponies going out in the boots we had to wear, very heavy boots with studs on them and then you'd thick socks and then your shin guards under the socks and most of the Celtic players then got cotton wool and stuck it inside the shin guards. So obviously the pace was nothing like today; they wear sandshoes nowadays compared to what we were wearing.

MATT LYNCH   I don't think the football today compares to the football of those years, when you wouldn't pass down a street or a piece of green grass where the boys weren't playing football. You can hardly get them to play football in school now. Then every boy played football. It was the only diversion they had.

People laugh at this. When I would be up at the park full-time training, it was all running round a track – walk the curved bit, and running on the straight. All running you know, and on a Thursday it was sprints. Somebody would say to John Crum, 'Go away and see if you can get us a ball.' Now they were sending him in because he was a favourite of the manager's; he was one of those big cocky Glasgow fellows and they sent him in because he was the manager's pet and would be likely to be granted a ball. And he would come out of this tunnel with the ball, and – imagine, professional footballers – everyone would be delighted! The joke was that we had to play behind the goal; and if by accident the ball was kicked onto the playing field, the head groundsman used to shout, 'Get the f*** off the f***ing park!' And he used to lift the ball and run off like a park-keeper protecting the flowerbeds.

Chapter Three

CROWDS

The late 1940s – 'the post-war boom' – saw huge crowds pouring into all the Glasgow grounds; to Partick's Firhill, Queen's Park's Hampden, Clyde's Shawfield and Third Lanark's Cathkin, as well as to Parkhead and Ibrox. Over the subsequent half-century Old Firm crowds have changed significantly – in look, nature and behaviour. The sedate Taylor-made crowds of the present are a far cry from the buzzing hordes who made 1940s Old Firm matches – win, lose or draw – an exciting spectatorial experience.

DOMINIC MURRAY   On a Saturday morning in Govan back in the '40s, you could feel the game building up. As soon as you woke up in the morning you'd go down and get to the corner and you'd see a boy with the colours on going up to somebody's house to get his mate to travel to the game. Round about ten o'clock you'd see wee groups; and at midday you'd see a right crowd going into the pubs and so on.

JACK JARDINE   If I go back to when I was a kid, and my brother worked on a Saturday morning – you'd laugh at it now, but it was clean up, get ready for him coming out of work on a Saturday morning, wait on him getting his dinner – 'Come on till we get up to this game.' I stayed in Govan; I stayed in Greenfield Street, which wasn't awful far away from Ibrox. You went up with your older brother and his pals, and you felt that the whole of Govan was going to that game; you'd be walking up and it was just a mass of blue and white. The amazing thing was the number of kids. I mean when they used to say there was a crowd of 40 or 50,000 – if the truth were known there were probably 70,000 there, because there were thousands of kids at the game, just waiting; and they just lifted them over.

BILL LAMOND   A buzz would be about the place. Ibrox was a lovely stadium even in those days; people forget it was a beautiful stadium before, it wasn't a heap that they reconstructed. You picked your spot; everybody had their spot at Ibrox because of the clearly directed passageways – you could meet somebody at Ibrox and say, 'See you at the top of Passageway 16.' Or the boys – all together – would be stood at the middle of Section 14.

JACK JARDINE   On the terraces you had your spot and that was that. That was your spot. And at that time everyone knew – you'd come up and your spot would be empty. You didn't need to book places – that was your spot on the terracing. You'd get up there, get your carry-oot laid down and that was you.

JOHN LAWSON   The old Jungle at Parkhead was like a hay-shed – full of holes; and I've seen many better hay-sheds in the farms around about where I live now. It was low, and the heat was terrible. Having said that, I've stood there in the same spot, year in, year out. The Jungle was a great place to watch football.

MATT LYNCH   Just after the war Parkhead had an eighty-odd thousand capacity; three sides standing. All you saw was caps and cigarette smoke. I didn't hear the crowd from the pitch, but there were voices. One of the programmes had a picture of me in the front with my graduation gown on. A fellow who taught with me told me: 'One of the funniest things I heard at Celtic Park was the day your photograph was on the programme and to put it mildly you weren't having too good a game. I don't know whether you were missing tackles or had played a bad ball but this fellow shouted out, 'Hey, Lynch! Where's your f***ing science noo!'

JIM COOKE   At that time I stood at Passageway 13 at Ibrox and watched from the terracing. One of the funny things about Passageway 13 was that there was one lad who, every time a Rangers player played the ball up towards us, 'kicked' the ball. So the ones that came there every Saturday knew to leave a space or they got a boot up the leg. It's true – he swung his feet out as if he was going to score a goal.

ADAM SHIELS   The majority of the time I always went to Passageway 16, the Rangers side of Parkhead, because it's on the Hamilton side. It was always the same people who stood there, game after game. Across the passageway was a crowd from Castlemilk, and we used to kid and joke with these chaps; their lassies were there, and my brother started to go to their dances with one of their lassies; he's married to her now. We used to go down to Castlemilk to their football nights out. You'd go in and you'd get your couple of pints; and the next thing you'd see the guy going out. He'd come back about 40 minutes later and plonk down big cardboard boxes right in the middle of the dance–floor – fish suppers and chicken suppers for everyone in the hall!

JACK JARDINE   You used to get these people – we called them the '20-minute mob'. Twenty minutes to go, they opened the gates. Nowadays, that's a signal for them all going out; then it was a signal for them all coming in! See if you were standing near the back, then with 20 minutes to go you would be getting crushed, because people were coming in all over the place. Now it's the opposite. That says volumes about present-day football, eh?

Memories of the '50s have a similar feel: big crowds happy to turn up for fixtures that, pre-Europe, were little more than domestic tiffs. In the '60s European football was on offer, but the feel of crush and sway remained.

51

GEORGE MOORE   When I went as a boy – I'm talking about round about 1956 – it was a different atmosphere entirely. You used to go to Firhill or somewhere on a Saturday and if you weren't there by two o'clock you wouldn't get in. If it was a smaller club you'd get the young boys running round at half-time to see how many goals they scored in that half, you know.

MARGARET DEVLIN   Before the season tickets you just went and paid your way, and it was always the same people who sat round about. It got to the stage where if you weren't there one week they'd say things like, 'Where were you? Are you all right?' Maybe you'd just gone to a different part of the ground for some reason. But you became like a family within a family.

HUGH FERRIE   I always sat in the same seat in the stand, immediately behind the directors' box. There was a couple from Paisley, Mr and Mrs Brennan, and they always kept a seat for me. I remember one day – I didn't get very excited during a game, but I had made some rather critical comments about Bobby Lennox, and this woman in front of me turned round and said, 'I think I should tell you, I'm Mrs Lennox . . .'

JAMES DUNBAR   The crowds were very different because people drank; people used to take their carry-out and their glass in the top pocket to pour the whisky and the beer into; when you were small if someone scored a goal the booze all went up into the air and you got covered in it and you went home reeking of whisky and beer and your mother thought you'd been on the razz. It was totally different – much more a masculine domain than now. I was under ten then; at that time I had to sit on a crush barrier, and I can remember my backside being frozen many a time from sitting at the top of Hampden or at Celtic Park. It was just as well the barriers at Celtic Park were wooden.

DAVID PALMER   In the 1960s getting there early was one thing – you had to get there a lot earlier than you do now. If you were on the terraces it was pretty essential to get a crush barrier to sit on top of, because otherwise you wouldn't be able to see. So as far as I remember I used to turn up about an hour and a half before kick-off and make sure that I got a perch, so I could see what was going on.

COLIN GLASS   In the north-eastern enclosure at Ibrox, where most of the singing used to be, I used to stand with my back against a crush barrier, because when Rangers scored the celebrations were quite exuberant, and you wouldn't be caught in the crowd surging forward if your back was at a barrier. If you were leaning against the front of it you could get your ribs crushed.

For those too small to see over the adult-sized bodies that made up the bulk of the crowd, other activities were on offer.

JOHN BUTTERFIELD   Collecting autographs came in the late '60s for me. I can remember I used to write to the clubs and they would send me photocopies of all the autographs. Love Street was always very good for getting autographs, because the pavilion was some distance from the entrance, and you could always manage to pester the players as they approached the pavilion. I can remember waiting endlessly to get autographs. I remember Jimmy Johnstone in a leather jacket – all the players wore Marvin Gaye-type leather jackets. Jimmy Johnstone stole my pen! He took my pen to sign an autograph and gave it away to someone else.

JOHN GARDNER   When we were kids we made a fortune by going to Ibrox and collecting ginger-bottles and beer-bottles. We got ourselves a carrot-bag – meshy, flexi, good for carrying bottles. We'd go to the game and we'd look for people who would lift us over the turnstile, or for a fat man who would push you under the turnstile. The bigger the beer-belly, the quicker you got in. We'd pick our sides and we'd just scout around, looking for the Irn Bru or the McEwan's beer bottles. You got threepence for an Irn Bru bottle, tuppence for a beer bottle. At big games, the supporters wouldn't go down to the loos; they'd stay on the terracing. You learned quickly to empty the bottles, never to sample them.

JACK PRIOR My old man had only one leg – he used to go up and sit in the stand, and he ended up with one of the wee invalid cars. You never see them anymore, but they used to park them, rows and rows of them, round the track at Hampden. I used to squeeze into the old man's motor to get into the game if I'd no ticket; stuffed into that daft wee motor. It was only a three-wheeler, too, and my old man was a big man. Seeing us trying to squeeze into it . . . Those were the days.

JOE SHEVLIN There was no catering in grounds at that time. In those days it was a macaroon bar, a pie, a Bovril. You could come to the ground with lager and beers; they used to bring in cartons of ten or 12. They used to carry them in quite openly because there was no law to stop this; and the place was littered with cans at time up.

JOHN BUTTERFIELD I remember the guys selling the macaroon bars, the spearmint chewing-gum – beech-nut chewing-gum. And the *official* programme – as if there was an unofficial one.

DAVID PALMER It was very different in the '60s. Those were the days when they still had massive terracing. I remember the sheer excitement, the volume of people and noise at matches in those days. The Ibrox Disaster put an end to that kind of stadium and changes had to be made; there's never been the same kind of atmosphere since. It's very civilised, but it doesn't send the same shivers down your spine as the place did in the 1960s.

Fashions on the terraces have altered with time; just as on the park, different times have brought different styles.

GEORGE MacLEOD After the war when you went to games you would just see – well, it's like you see on Pathé News or something – huge crowds of men in bunnets, overcoats.

ALEX BELL Back in the days when Ibrox would take maybe 100,000 people, all the old men would be decked out in the bunnets; that's the amazing thing when you watch these old pieces of black-and-white footage, everybody but everybody's got a bunnet on their head. The whole hat trade must have taken a plummet because it's never seen now.

GEORGE MOORE I used to have to wear wellies when I went to games as a boy in the '50s. I've still got the red rings round my legs. A big blooming parish coat, with my shorts on, and wellies. We were very poor round about Parkhead, you know!

GEORGE MacLEOD By the time you get on to the '60s it was still a collar and tie job; you did get guys wearing this very sharp gear, this *Top of the Pops* stuff, but basically it was the suits – the narrow lapels, the short backs, the thin-collared white shirt, the self-coloured tie.

TOMMY HYNDMAN The '70s fashions – oh my god! – crombie coats, in the middle of summer, with the wee red hankies, Harrington jackets, those mad Birmingham bags with the pockets down the side, the Kung-Fu jumpers. About the same time we used to wear the workmen's safety helmets, painted in the club colours with the number of your favourite player and all that; maybe even the names of the whole team; it depended on how big your head was, right enough. The Wrangler denim jackets with a flag cut out and put into the back-space. Platforms. How anybody ever ran to catch the game with those platforms on I'll never know. If you were in the Jungle, and maybe you were down at the front because you were still quite young, you'd get the old guys behind you saying, 'Hey you – get aff that ladder!'

STEVEN GALL Flares. High waisters and flares. The red and the brown Kojak jersey. Then you got the Bay City Roller material. The big boots; I had them. The Bay City Roller gear was always tartan. I had the white denim trousers with the tartan all the way down the sides, and my granny bought me these hideous white shoes with the tartan tongue in them.

NEIL McDERMOTT   Back then there weren't so many people wore colours. Nowadays you're the odd one out if you don't have colours on. And of course the big thing in the last few years has been the growth of these replica shirts. Everyone seems to have them now.

JOHN LARKIN   In our day, the kids were never really allowed to wear the strips – my mum and dad would always say, 'Wear them, but don't go out with them on.' It was too dangerous.

TOMMY HYNDMAN   What's really taken a jump is the massive banners – you see them everywhere. I mean there's quite a few really really good banners. Traditionally with Celtic fans it's been the Irish tricolour with the name of the club that made them, but you're even getting sponsored now to make them, sponsored banners.

STEVEN GALL   The one that the Belvedere Supporters Club takes is an absolute belter – green and white checks with Belvedere written across it. It does cover a lot of square footage. They pass it from the front to the back – and it's as though the banner's hovering, fluttering over the fans' heads.

The present requires all-seated crowds; an appropriately sedate atmosphere seems to have ensued.

SANDRA LEWSEY   The atmosphere now is not as good as it was. I think sitting is much more comfortable – but standing you get a much, much better atmosphere. You're standing when you score, of course, but you know you've got to sit back down again, and it does take something away from it. It's more civilised, now – on the terraces men were drinking and men used to do the toilet in the cans and throw them, and it was disgusting. That aspect of things, the facilities, are so good now.

FRANK GLENCROSS   There was a lot of camaraderie in the '60s which doesn't exist now. You'd talk to the person beside you. Nowadays you'd be lucky to find anybody to talk to in the same way. If you're sitting beside someone you can't get on with then that's it.

DOMINIC MURRAY   The trouble with an all-seater stadium is that in the old days if you had five or six idiots standing next to you you could move over a wee bit and get away from them. But if you're sitting there's no getting away. They say report it to the stewards but you can't; you're sitting there and they'll say – 'We'll see you outside, we'll see you again.'

COLIN LAMOND   At Ibrox they don't want the old type of fervour; they want calm and dignity.

Do you know who the Copland Nutter is? I think he's from Fernhill – he's a small guy, with glasses. He must have a season ticket at the Copland Road end, and he's been in with a lambeg drum, bashing it and running up and down the stairs and basically conducting the whole stand. Now he's been talked to a couple of times by the authorities within the stadium for being too boisterous and leaving his seat all the time – they're not happy with that.

STEF JARDINE   You've got the likes of the Govan Stand now; the only time you know they're actually there is when you see a fag getting lit; they're just wee cardboard cut-outs until a fag gets lit. The enclosure are always saying, 'Can you hear the Copland sing?' and all that, trying to incite them into a song. The Copland Nutter – if he was in Europe, the club would pay him. People like Barcelona, or some of those Italian mobs – they pay guys to get the crowd up into a frenzy. The Copland Nutter's trying to do the same thing and they're trying to stop him.

NEIL McDERMOTT   The crowd has got younger at Celtic Park as the years have passed. If you look at the pictures of the crowds from the '40s – if they show you a picture of behind the goals at Parkhead, Ibrox, Hampden – then what you see are cloth caps galore – men – whereas now the majority of the crowd at Celtic Park recently has been young people. I think the older heads in the crowd have voted with their minds and feet and they're not going to watch it. The young seem to have this greater tolerance level. The rest of us – we're not going to watch mince.

HARVEY BEATON The atmosphere then and now? It's night and day. You can't start hugging and kissing somebody in the next seat, can you? You maybe give somebody a hug or give somebody a clap but if you're all standing up and everybody's jumping about – it was just entirely different. I don't know if it's maybe that you're getting old, but any time you go abroad and you go to certain grounds where there's standing, then you seem to still have that atmosphere. There was a lot more freedom.

SANDY STRANG Even in the European games at Ibrox you feel the change. Watching the Leeds United game, a big game, you felt that the theatre had gone out of it. The crowd was still shouting and was still behind the side but it was a different experience. It is a different era; but to go along to the blue room or to come out and have your bluenose burger and walk in neat straight lines down the road back to your video or whatever, is a less human experience and a less celebratory experience than football was, and I'm convinced that a lot has been lost. Fans don't want to sign up for a plastic bucket seat in a family enclosure. Many of the people who were real football people – sadly perhaps, because maybe it's a function of the Scottish male – felt that it wasn't intended to be a family experience. Football was where the chap went out and became a different person – sometimes an unpleasant person – and he took a lot from that which he was able to put back in in terms of his day-to-day life thereafter. I feel that's irrevocably lost.

JOE SHEVLIN I thought the crowds were a lot happier then than now. They filled the passages, you'd no stewards, and the regimentation you've got now you didn't need. Nowadays you've got stewards all up the passageways, all round the ground, outside, inside; you go to an away game and they stop you in the street, they search you before you go into the ground, once you go into the ground you're shepherded into a place. The enjoyment's all gone out of that. In the old days you went to the game, you saw the game, you were with your mates – and that was it. Real football.

Chapter Four

HOME and AWAY
1955–1965

The late '50s and early '60s saw National Service for all, including footballers. Not only did Rangers and Celtic players have to endure a bout of the GI Blues; they also found themselves, on their return, signed up for National Service of a different kind with the establishment of European competitions. From the off, these added a new dimension and excitement to the Scottish game; the Celtic support, enduring a long, lean period of schlock around the clock, needed it more than most. For Rangers supporters, times were easier. Although the Iron Curtain rusted there appeared from behind it a team which played with vivid beauty in the first five years of the '60s; a sweet soul music orchestrated, of course, by the remarkable figure of the then Slim Jim Baxter.

BILLY RITCHIE   In the late 1950s we – Rangers – were an ageing team; if not aged. Ian McColl was still playing – he was the last of the post-war team. I took over from George Niven about 1957. I was fortunate not to play in the League Cup final of 1957. I had actually played in the semi-final against Brechin but that Saturday in October I finished up in the Royal Scots Fusiliers at Ayr; my National Service. I finished up in Cyprus for seven months – it was the time of the trouble in Cyprus. I never saw a ball for a while. We were treated no differently from the ordinary soldiers; no Elvis Presley stuff at all.

The final Billy Ritchie missed was the high spot of the decade for the green half of the city. For Rangers it was a massive humiliation; for Celtic fans it remains one of the mythical days: 'Hampden in the sun – Celtic 7 Rangers 1'.

SEAN FALLON   At that time the Rangers believed in man-marking; we played wide, with two wingers, Mochan and Tully; their backs were Shearer and Caldow and they went wide. Rangers were after signing a centre-half by name Valentine. And the boy was exposed, totally exposed. We could have got a bus through the middle of their defence.

DOMINIC MURRAY   My uncle Andy – he was a Rangers supporter – had just finished flitting to Castlemilk. I went up there and had my dinner and he said he'd to go and get his mates; they were all Rangers boys, all five of them; he worked in the Larkfield Garage as an electrician. The game started – bang, bang – Celtic two up. I'm sitting there like a dummy. The Celtic End was going mad; from the first goal it never stopped. 3–0, 3–1, 4–1, 5–1; and this wee bloke John says to my uncle Andy, 'I canny take any more of this. I'll see you Monday.' And Andy says, 'I'll come too.' So I had to leave and all. The five of us jumped in a taxi, went down to Paisley Road Toll. As we got out a wee paperboy shouts, 'Hey, John – were you at the game?' 'Aye,' John says, 'We were getting beat 5–1. Terrible.' The boy says, 'No, it's 6–1.' John says, 'Stop! Stop!' So he said cheerio and we walked along to Houston Street where my uncle Andy's ma stayed. We're going up the close and another guy shouts up the close, 'Were you at the game today?' Andy says, 'Aye, they got beat 6–1.' And the guy says, 'Naw, it's 7–1. Fernie's scored with a penalty.' And Andy says, 'I'm not speaking to anybody else today.'

  . . . you and that f***ing football . . .

LIAM MacLUSKEY I worked for the Co-op Building Department at Shieldhall. My boss had asked me on the Friday if I would work on the Saturday. My best friend Jimmy Fletcher, who was a Rangers supporter, said that Celtic were going to get hammered and I was better working. We had nearly all the work done by ten past two, and I was egged on to ask the foreman to let me away. He said, 'You and that f***ing football . . . away you go.' I went to the Bothy; as I ran out Jimmy said, 'Do you want my hanky to greet in?' The game was 20 minutes started when I got into Hampden Park. 7–1! I'll give Jimmy his due – he turned up for work on the Sunday.

FRANK MOOTY I had left Cleland and was down in Yorkshire, down the pits. There was the radio, the wireless as we called it. This lad in the pit was a bit of an electrician and he said, 'Right, come round to my house.' He fixed up a wire at the back of my wireless to earth it through the window with the poker; he tied the wire round the poker and stuck it into the ground; that's what he called earthing. So we were sitting and listening to the game; there was that much crackle on the wireless I thought I was hearing things. It was glorious.

STUART DANIELS The 7–1 débâcle? I was only ten years of age. I had a big, big bag and I collected a load of bottles because there were plenty that got flung that day. I think even the police were throwing bottles. I came back down to Kinning Park and met my father coming out of the pub. He says, 'Where were you today?' I says, 'I was at Hampden, Dad. I've collected about 50 beer bottles . . .' And he gave me a doing. It wasn't for collecting the beer bottles and being there; it was because of Celtic scoring seven goals.

JOHNNY HUBBARD I was in all the record-breaking Rangers teams. Celtic beat us 7–1. Aberdeen beat us 6–0. But I did score a hat-trick against Celtic in January 1955, so I got forgiven. I was on television that night, on STV, with Charlie Tully, and he was going on about the 7–1. I told him that we'd missed eight good chances.

. . . of course it was only a one-off – Rangers regrouped and we lost the Ne'erday game . . .

EUGENE MacBRIDE In 1957 I was in Holland. I was actually shovelling coke with a great big fork, wearing clogs. Somebody came up to me and said Celtic beat Rangers 7–1, and I thought it was a joke. It was no joke and I jumped out of the clogs; I literally jumped out of them. Of course it was only a one-off; Rangers regrouped and we lost the Ne'erday game.

Rangers' general domination on the domestic front meant that they were quicker off the mark than Celtic in going into Europe. Even they had hesitated; like the English F.A., Rangers were not sure what to make of the invitation to enter the first European Cup of 1955–56, and the invitation – and the distinction of being the first British side to play in Europe – passed to a Hibs team who, though a couple of years past their best, reached the semi-finals. The following season, however, Rangers were in the draw as Champions of Scotland.

Celtic did not qualify for Europe until 1962. While they were waiting they continued to play friendlies and took part in other impromptu European competitions, but for Rangers it was the real McCoy. Within five or six years they contested their first European final.

BILLY RITCHIE We played Nice in our first year. We flew first class – it was tremendous for us as ordinary working boys – a wee bit awesome. We beat them at Ibrox 2–1. The second game was at Nice. We were thinking, hot, hot, hot; they said it only rained so many days in a year there. Well, it rained all the time we were there.

IAN McCOLL We flew out to play them on the Wednesday and it was pouring down with rain. So we flew back home and played a game on the Saturday. Then we flew back the next Wednesday – it was still raining, but we played anyway, in mud up to here – and we lost 2–1. Then we had a toss of the coin and we lost, so the third game was in Paris.

BILLY RITCHIE The following season we were in France again; at St Etienne. By then the idea was setting in that it was really no different from anything else; that foreign players have only got two legs, two arms and a head like anybody else. But in the second round we had to play AC Milan and we got a hammering.

. . . the year Rangers made an A-R-S-E of themselves in Europe . . .

BILL LAMOND One of the most vivid memories I've got is of the year Frankfurt played Madrid at Hampden in the final – the famous 7–3 game. That year Rangers played Anderlecht, Red Star, Sparta and then Eintracht in the semi-finals. From the first letters of these teams it became known as the year Rangers made an A-R-S-E of themselves in Europe, since Eintracht beat them 12–4 on aggregate.

I remember going when they played Sparta in a third game at Highbury. It was a smashing game – I think Rangers won 3–1 or 3–2. Sammy Baird scored two goals that night – he was a big, straight guy, a good, big runner. I remember the whistle going and I remember running onto the park. There were three or four of us; we picked up Sammy Baird, got him on our shoulders. He's saying, 'Put us down! Put us down!' – though he was obviously quite excited about it all. Once he saw we weren't going to cause him any harm he was happy for us to hoick him round Highbury. In the end *we* had to say, 'I think we'll let you down now Sam . . .'

JOHN LARKIN I saw that 1960 final, Real Madrid against Eintracht – I was standing on two tin cans.

HUGH TONER The European Cup final of 1960 showed Glasgow at its best – 135,000 there, you could say 130,000 neutrals, and they stayed right to the end to cheer both teams, even though Eintracht had taken 12 goals off Rangers in the semi-finals.

BILL LAMOND Rangers did get to the Fairs' Cup final in 1961. That was the first final. A lot of people forget that one.

One of my most abiding memories is going down to

Molineux and seeing them play down there in the semi-final. We just took over the town that day; we went to the game at night and the whole bank behind one of the goals was just awash with red, white and blue. That was an atmosphere worth sampling.

. . . that was our first run-in with Rangers supporters going crazy in the streets . . .

DOUG BAILLIE   I remember it mainly because that was our first run-in with Rangers fans going crazy on the streets. We saw these Rangers supporters coming down the street giving it 'The Sash' or whatever the thing was in those days; it was a bit of a laugh. But then we got back to the hotel and found everything had been turned over and it was Rangers supporters who had done it. I don't know whether they knew; I wasn't *that* bad a player.

I went to Fiorentina for the final. We went to Viareggio for a beach holiday before the game; we were totally sunburned and most of us could hardly move. That tells you something about the approach! It was a two-legged affair. I don't remember the scores now but I suspect Fiorentina must have won at Ibrox because the Italian ice-cream vans were turned upside down on the Copland Road when the punters came out. Kurt Hamrin was their star – number 7, a Swede, played with his stockings down over his boots, nobody could get the ball off him.

Celtic's involvement was more faltering in its pace. This was not a matter of choice.

NEIL McDERMOTT   Because of the seven lean years Celtic's involvement in Europe got off to a slow start. The first encounters with European teams I remember were in a thing called the Friendship Cup; three or four Scottish teams played three or four French teams. A team called Sédan came to Celtic Park and it was anything but friendly.

JOHN LARKIN   An early memory of mine is when Real Madrid came over. Eighty thousand there – for a friendly! We wouldn't let the other team go home. I've got a picture; somebody must have taken a picture from the balcony of the Central Hotel, and you see all these scarves and faces. This must have been getting on for 11 at night. Di Stefano, Puskas, all the others who'd played at Hampden not long before – it was fantastic.

Something wonderful had happened at Ibrox in the close season of 1960; for the princely sum of £17,500 Rangers acquired a player who, at that stage of his wayward existence, could still be called Slim Jim Baxter without irony. Around him was built a team that occupies, in the minds of Rangers supporters, the same space that the Lisbon Lions have to themselves in the minds of Celts; a team that is held in more affection than the Cup Winners' Cup-winning team of 1972.

Baxter was a hedonist, an over-indulger who would very probably not have been tolerated in Struth's team. He excited the crowd; he also excited the imagination. An Easterner at the heart of the bastion of West of Scotland Protestantism, his speciality was trickery that was designed to humiliate the opposition. When the opposition was Celtic, Rangers' fans loved it; when the opposition was Alan Ball, all Scots did. Slim Jim's nickname came to haunt him in his later years, when, Elvis-like, he was bloated with excess. With Presley, one endeavours to ignore the fat old man in the sequinned jumpsuit sweating on stage in favour of memories of the slimline Pelvis.

JOHN LAWSON   I'm one of these blokes – I'm not a bigot – I like to see good players in any team. My two sons said to me recently, 'What kind of a player was Baxter?' I said, 'Well, he couldnae head the ball, he couldnae tackle, he couldnae touch the ball with his right foot. . . he was one of the greatest players who ever played.'

BILLY RITCHIE   Watching Baxter from the back was the great thing; from the back he had this tremendous wiggle, the famous shimmy. Jim's going one way; they're coming towards him; he doesn't touch the ball, he just goes their way; and then all of a sudden it's as if somebody has dragged the player away and he goes through. It's true Jim couldn't tackle a fish supper.

But if you ever needed him – if you were ever in trouble – Jim was always in a space to get the ball.

DOUG BAILLIE   Jim was the most harem-scarem character I ever met in my life. He hadn't a care in the world. He used to come in in the morning and have a shower and suck a polo-mint before he even went in to the Rangers dressing-room, because he hadn't been home from the night before, he'd just made it in for training and no more – a terrible man. He never shut his face, that was the other thing; that Fife accent, sort of high-pitched; 'aye, aye, come on son, aye, aye, aye, give me the ball over here son, aye, aye, aye,' in this very, very strong Fife accent.

   . . . I'd go home from school and say, 'could I have a Jim Baxter hair-cut?'. . .

JOHN LARKIN   I used to idolise him – I know it's incredible, he was a Rangers player, but I used to wish he played for Celtic. I used to go home and say, 'Could I have a Jim Baxter haircut?' He was who you would want to play football like; and he looked the part.

ALEX BELL   I remember Baxter coming to Ibrox. To us at the time he looked like a real cornerboy kind of thing; the suits and all that, a style we weren't used to at Ibrox. His hair was terribly short at the time as he'd just come out the army and he had the Italian suits and the suede boots. We were going to the Dennistoun Palais and so on and soon we were wearing Italian suits as well. We had our hair cut really short; we used to go to an American shirt-maker way up at the top of Buchanan Street called Esquire's – so we thought we were the bees knees too.

   We would never go to the terraces wearing that stuff, though; it wasn't just that we might get a doing; it was that when we went out everything had to be just pristine; we'd go to the football and then just go straight home, get shaved, changed, spruced up and go out to the dancing, whatever the case might be.

CHARLIE GALLAGHER   There was one icy day in the early '60s when we were playing Rangers – it was so icy Bob Kelly tried to have the game called off, but it was played. And Baxter was on the top of his form; he was nutmegging everyone, and I mean everyone, we were all sliding about all over the place. It was like a humiliation game. You never forgot what he had done to you; he told you all about it.

NEIL McDERMOTT   Rangers were completely dominant. There was a spell when they seemed to win every game 3–0. And as soon as they went 2–0 up – it was then that I first heard the chant, 'Easy, Easy!' That really got to you.

JIMMY BROWN   What mustn't be forgotten is that Jim Baxter played in a fine team; it was no one-man band. It's another team I remember off by heart: Ritchie, Shearer, Caldow, Greig, McKinnon, Baxter, Henderson, McMillan, Millar, Brand and Wilson.

DOUG BAILLIE   I don't know if the rest of the side was underrated by comparison but Harry Davis was; he was the right-half, number 4. I was number 5 sometimes and Jim Baxter was number 6, and Ian McMillan was just ahead of big Harry. But Harry was the guy who was the workhorse for these guys; Baxter and McMillan were the luxury players who floated about, in and out the game; Harry was the one who got the ball for them and gave them the ball to do the business.

> *. . . 'well, if I hear you're there again,' he says, 'I'll break your f***ing neck' . . .*

ALEC WILLOUGHBY   A Rangers dressing-room in those days wasn't a place for the faint-hearted. I can remember very clearly one day after I'd played well at Ibrox I got the full treatment from the pals and the papers and whatnot. I came in on the Monday and was stripping beside Harold Davis and Harold said something about where was I at the weekend? I said I was at such-and-such a place – as a typical Glasgow boy – a particular party in a particular area. He said, 'Well, if I hear you're there again,' he says, 'I'll break your f***ing neck.' To which I turned round and I said, 'I can surely do what I want to do, because . . .' And he says,

'Why – do you think you're a good player?' And I says, 'Yes, I think I'm a good player. Most certainly. And so did Arthur Montford on Saturday night, and Rex Kingsley, and John McKenzie in the *Express*.' At that time these were the equivalents of the modern day Chick Youngs or Gerry McNees. And Harold grabbed me by the lapels of the jacket and just lifted me up off the floor, and he says to me, 'I'm going to tell you something, son; John McKenzie and Rex Kingsley don't play with you. I play with you. And I'll tell you when you're a good player.'

JACK JARDINE   Now I liked Baxter, he was an absolute hero of mine, but the real closeness to the players wasn't there any longer, because they started to buy players in. They started with Baxter from Raith Rovers, then wee McMillan from Airdrie, it was Colin Stein – it wasn't any longer the Brown, Young, Shaw, blah, blah, blah that you could rhyme off, it wasn't the players that you knew from Govan or from the Juniors and who would speak to you, it was bought-in players. That probably started weakening the other teams, the Hibs and the whatnot, and you really felt it was the money, the money started taking over. I don't know, the feeling for the team seemed to go.

After the 7–1 game came dreadful times for Celtic. It was the time when Sir Bob Kelly, the very model of the all-intrusive chairman, was more or less in charge of team affairs; his Kelly Kids bore little or no resemblance to the Busby Babes their nickname aped. But promising youngsters were there; a promising coach looked after them.

BILLY McNEILL   I signed for Celtic in 1957; I was farmed out to Blantyre Victoria for a year, and then I was called up. We had some smashing senior professional players. Big Jock Stein was there in fact; when I went to the reserve team, Jock had had an injury and he had been put in charge. We used to travel in and out of Lanarkshire to Celtic Park; big Jock went to Burnbank. We would walk into Tollcross Road with him to get the bus. There was an unwritten rule: if big Jock's bus didn't come first then we had to wait until his bus came. We used to sit and blether and learn, and he left a big influence on a lot of us. But of course if his bus came first then he was on it and away.

CHARLIE GALLAGHER   This was the era when Bob Kelly used to run the team, and he would chop and change the team for no apparent reason. We used to be able to tell the team half way through the week. If Bob Kelly walked in through the main entrance at Celtic Park and he walked right past you, you knew you weren't playing on the Saturday. If he said 'Good morning!' then you knew you were playing.

   . . . Bob Kelly ran the team, and he treated it as if it was a Boys' Guild . . .

JOHN LAWSON   Bob Kelly ran the team, and he treated it as if it was a Boys' Guild. It was a rough time. My wife said to me the other night, 'When we were first married, you came in every Saturday with your face tripping you, getting beat by the likes of Albion Rovers and Third Lanark and these teams.' Celtic have been through rough, rough periods; they went from – what, 1957 until – what, 1965 and never won anything.

GEORGE SHERIDAN   The team was dreadful, absolutely dreadful. It was the time of the Kelly Kids, and they were all far too young. Stein had gone off to Dunfermline. The forwards – they couldn't burst a poke. The crowd felt that they were living in Rangers' shadow and the smallest success was grasped upon. I can remember a midweek game, and at the end of the game Celtic had actually won a cup. Everybody started going over the wee wall at the Jungle, on to the park across to the tunnel, all going mad to see this trophy. And this, believe it or not, was celebrating winning the Glasgow Cup. Against Third Lanark.

DAVID POTTER   Celtic were in the wars. I was there at the time when they played Queen of the South – the second Saturday of the 1963 season. There was really quite a lot of crowd disturbance – I remember getting 'dispersed' by the mounted police and there were demonstrations against Bob Kelly. He had wisely gone to see the reserve match at Dumfries.

   In 1964–65 I often went to see them, including a 3–1 victory over Rangers at Parkhead in lashing rain. I enjoyed the sight of incredulous fans embracing each other. Celtic was more important than sex – some admission that, for a sixteen-year-old. I had many chances to go out with girls, but needed money to finance my Celtic obsession. By New Year I was approaching the clinically depressed stage when Murdoch ballooned a penalty over the Ibrox bar, and rock bottom was the 2–1 defeat to Hearts at Parkhead in mid-January on a cold wet day with rain dripping in through the holes in the Jungle roof. Hearts fans outnumbered and outshouted the home support for the first time in history. At the end of January, though, on the day of Winston Churchill's funeral, they beat Aberdeen 8–0 and the next day came the announcement of Jock Stein's return.

In Europe, Bob Kelly's tactical influence led Celtic into trouble on one celebrated occasion – a semi-final against MTK in Budapest – but, considering their inexperience and their ongoing domestic travails, they did not fare too badly in their early travels.

NEIL McDERMOTT   When they started their real involvement in European ties, Celtic's home record was superb. At one point they must have played seven or eight home games – we're talking about teams like Slovan Bratislava and Zagreb Dinamo and even Liverpool – and it was a case of the other team nil, nil, nil. The Celtic song came out in about 1962, so you always had this big build-up over the tannoy and it always ended up with the Celtic song, with the crowd all geed up by that time. Sometimes you'd be terrified watching these fellows before the match started. They looked so good, they'd murder Celtic . . . but it was the opposite way round once the tackling started.

   . . . we used to get the ball and try to attack, diving in all over the place . . .

CHARLIE GALLAGHER   Valencia was a Fairs' Cities Cup tie. We were completely intimidated. I don't know whether you've ever been in the Valencia Stadium – it's a big round bowl, and with a big crowd it was like a bull-ring. We were completely out of our depth. The Spanish players were holding the ball and throwing it about and we were running and trying to chase them instead of just standing back as we did in later years. We used to get the ball and try to attack, diving in all over the place.

JOHN HUGHES I remember going to Zagreb the next year – the communist countries were dreadful. Jim Brogan was always clowning about in the street and and he decided to fall down in the street and get people to help him. So we stood by and he went down on the ground. And people just ignored him, simply because they didn't want to get involved. And we were howling, watching him; eventually he just had to get up. We were knotting ourselves; people were just terrified; people used to just walk and never smile, and they were always going somewhere with a purpose. Then it was Budapest for the semi-final . . .

CHARLIE GALLAGHER Budapest was an absolute disaster. We knew nothing. For a team to be leading 3–0 and go away from home and get beat 4–0 in a semi-final . . . The other team wasn't even a good side. Kelly put out the standard Celtic Park 11 and the attitude was, go out and enjoy yourselves. I tell you, when you're getting beat 4–0 there's not much enjoyment.

Curiously, the 'Baxter team' – apart from the Fairs' Cup run that led to the defeat by Fiorentina – did not have an outstanding European record. The year Rangers narrowly lost a tie against Milan after Baxter had broken his leg in Vienna is regarded by many fans as a year that Rangers might have won the European Cup – and, more importantly, allowed them to avoid all the grief of having to listen to Celtic fans going on about how they did it first.

BILLY RITCHIE One year we had to go to Sweden. We were playing an East German team, Vorwaerts. Their park was just by the Wall; I remember going up to have a look at the Wall, and the sirens went up, and dogs and that came out. What with Checkpoint Charlie and all that Vorwaerts couldn't come across to Britain, so we had to play in Malmo. Over there the fog came down and I couldn't see anything. I was running about trying to keep warm and Caldow came running over and he says, 'What are you doing out here, Billy? The game's finished.' I had been standing there not able to see anything! We had to start again in the morning, at nine o'clock in the morning. It was like being back at school.

. . . the Twist . . . was just coming to the fore and I think John Greig might have been the first man to do it in Russia . . .

DOUG BAILLIE I signed in August 1960 and I travelled all the time with them. We were one of the first teams to go to Russia. The Russian trip was a famous trip because everywhere we went the Russians kept filling everyone full of vodka and having sing-songs and making speeches. I think the Twist – the Chubby Checker thing – was just coming to the fore here at that particular time and I think John Greig may have been the first man ever to do it in Russia; on a table at an aftermatch reception.

BILLY RITCHIE 1962–63 we had a nightmare game against Spurs – they beat us 5–2. The usual Scotland–England thing. Then the year after that it was Real Madrid. Gento and Puskas and di Stefano. They hammered us.

ALEC WILLOUGHBY Real Madrid were still the kingpins of Europe; I had seen them play in the final at Hampden in 1959–60; Jim Forrest and I had stood in the schoolboys' enclosure. To have watched that and then to find yourselves three years later walking out at the Bernabeu against them . . . and although you're a Glasgow boy, you're a cocky, confident wee lad, when you saw these guys play . . .
The game got started – a nine-o'clock kick-off – a very humid, sticky, Spanish evening – a great atmosphere. And we were three down in 15 minutes. And I always remember Jim Forrest bending down to centre the ball after the third goal; and I look across and of course George McLean is in the number 10 jersey, I'm in the number 8, Forrest is in the number 9; and I see George's features because Forrest has bent down to centre the ball. Now the white V of my jersey is actually pale blue with the sweat; Forrest is wringing wet under the oxters and on the chest with the hairs coming through; and here is big George – 'Dandy' as he was known to us – looking as if he had just stepped out of a

bandbox. So me being me, I says to him, 'Listen you, you big f***ing so-and-so; we're three down here and you've not moved ten yards either side of that half-way line.' 'I know, wee man,' he says, 'but what a view I've got.'

STEPHEN MURRAY   One good story I heard about George McLean was that one night he was coming out of Ibrox and a wee boy came up to him and asked for his autograph. McLean signed. When the wee boy looked down at his book McLean had written 'Pele'. 'You're no Pele!' the wee boy said. McLean said: 'Naw. But I played like him the day.'

GEORGE MacLEOD   In 1964–65 we had a good run – Red Star Belgrade, Rapid Vienna, Inter Milan. A great run. But a disappointing season, too, because of Baxter's leg; I always felt he was never the same again.

. . . that day Jimmy took everything but the gate-money . . .

ALEC WILLOUGHBY   Baxter was a great player. But if you look at his career at Ibrox it was only five years really; he broke his leg in the Prater Stadium in Vienna – one of the finest one-man performances I've ever seen. Rapid were nobody's pushover; they were possible winners of the European Cup, with six internationals in their side, I think, and here's a guy from Hill o' Beith in Fife dictating the game as if he was a conductor with a baton. Taking the piss? That day Jimmy took everything but the gate-money.

WILLIE JOHNSTON   Vienna was the best game I ever saw Baxter play. The Vienna players were after him because he was taking the piss; he was putting it through the boy's legs and coming back and putting it through again, and the boy did him.

ALEC WILLOUGHBY   After Vienna we were drawn against Inter. The game in Milan they won 3–1 and at that time 3–1 wasn't a bad result. When we brought them back to Ibrox Jim Forrest scored early to make it 1–0; we played in all-white that night, a frosty night. That brought it back to 3–2 – the margin over the two games was very tight.

Between 1957 and 1965 Celtic won nothing of any note. In 1957 the important thing was the score; in 1965, when they won the Cup, Jock Stein had arrived and the important thing was the meaning. Celtic were back; their best players would stay; a new era was about to begin. The glee that surrounded the thumping of Rangers in 1957 seems typical of an era when defeating Rangers meant Celtic had had a good season. Relief was the order of the day when the Cup was won in 1965, but that was soon over; Celtic, and Scottish, eyes were turning towards further horizons. Stein, like Souness later, knew that to win at home was no longer enough.

EDDIE McGRAW I think it was brilliant that Celtic appointed Stein. Though the headlines were 'Celtic Appoint Protestant Manager'.

SEAN FALLON I worked side by side with Stein. My job was to bring in young players – I was in charge of the reserve team. McNeill was already there. I brought in Gemmell and Craig. I brought Auld back from Birmingham. At that time we had a young side and they were playing mile-a-minute; they had no old head there to stand on the ball and slow things up. I saw Auld and made a deal with the club for £11,000. I spoke to Bertie – he was desperate to get back to Glasgow. All he wanted was the deposit on a house, which was next to nothing.

Our goalkeeper at that time was John Fallon – a tremendous keeper in training, he'd hands like shovels – but to be fair to the boy, in the games, John was very nervous. I'd been told on the grapevine Ronnie Simpson was being let go as player-manager to Berwick Rangers. He was an experienced goalkeeper – he'd won English badges with Newcastle United – there was no way the youngsters were going to get on to an experienced player like Simpson. I got him for £2,000; Ronnie was through within an hour.

. . . the more we practised, the luckier we got . . .

CHARLIE GALLAGHER Stein had been to Italy to study Herrera, and the training changed right away. We still trained hard, we still did our running round the park, but we saw more and more of the ball and we started to practise things.

People would say, 'That was a lucky goal', – but it would have been tried in training. It was the old Gary Player motto – the more we practised the luckier we got. Before Stein came we never practised anything.

BRIAN McBRIDE My first memory of Celtic was going to the 1965 Scottish Cup final. Before then, because I lived near Ibrox I was actually a bit of a closet Rangers fan, and my father came in one day with tickets for the schoolboys' enclosure, and he said that any Celtic supporters could join him at this. So my brother and I went to see Celtic beating Dunfermline 3–2, Billy McNeill scoring the winner with a header, and that was really the start of Celtic's great era with Jock Stein and all the success they had over the next ten years.

DAVID POTTER I remember the Cup final of 1965 vividly. I remember thinking that it was Tommy Gemmell that had scored the winning goal, because I just saw a flash of golden hair, and my father said, 'Billy McNeill,' and all the crowd around were saying, 'Billy McNeill, Billy McNeill.' And I remember the last nine minutes – my insides were churning because I was at the stage where I couldn't possibly believe that Celtic could win something because we had become so inured to disappointment. I remember we got back into the centre of town and went into Lewis's where you could get a good tea at that time; it was very emotional. I remember just being so relieved that they'd won something. At last.

CHARLIE GALLAGHER Wee Bertie Auld and I still talk about that final, because big Jock had taken us aside earlier in the year and told us, 'You'll never play in the same team because the two of you are too similar. We need different types of players.' And so on. Anyway, the Cup final came and I was playing inside right and wee Bertie was playing outside left. And both of us had good games. So were were all presented with our medals and we went into the dressing-room. In the old changing-room at Hampden there was a wee spot, a separate compartment for trainers and managers and so on. And big Jock was sitting there. And wee Bertie says to me, 'Here, give us your medal.' I said, 'What do you want it for?' He says, 'Just give me your medal.' And he walked into the compartment and he said, 'Here you are, Jock – what about the two f***ing players that can't play together?' And he threw the medals at him. I looked across and I could see the wee smile on Stein's face.

. . . the Gorbals was a very vibrant part of the city in those days . . .

BILLY McNEILL The Gorbals was a very vibrant part of the city in those days and very much a Celtic stronghold and I remember being on the bus – we were heading back into town to the Central Hotel for the celebrations. The bus driver spent his time getting into town dodging the fans who were trying to stop the bus. The area round about Central Station was blocked off for probably a couple of hours that night. There was an incredible euphoria about because it had been such a long time.

Chapter Five

TRAVEL

The 1950s saw a huge increase in away travel; improved roads and vehicles, as well as the end of the traditional obligation to work on Saturday mornings, left fans free to follow their teams around Scotland. Scotland was a good place to go away in at that time. Even if roads were slow by modern standards, the distances from Glasgow to most grounds were not large. Aberdeen required a special effort, but almost everywhere else was in easy reach and many sides were – and are – situated within the central corridor.

Supporters' buses were a great boom industry of the 1950s. They usually began informally; a group of fans getting together to avoid having to travel through congested cities by public transport; they would often travel to home games only. They were, however, conducted with strict formality. Supporters' clubs borrowed Trade Union terminology to name their office-bearers – Bus Convener, Assistant Bus Convener. They were usually fairly well-disciplined, though this varied from club to club and every bus had its characters.

In the '60s more and more fans – especially the younger boys – eschewed the cosy formalities of the supporters' club buses in favour of the heady joys of travelling individually, usually by train. Posters all over stations gave the times of the 'Football Specials' – Saturday-only trains usually comprised of old and battered rolling-stock that made the Underground trains of the period appear luxurious and which were nicknamed cattle-trucks. When they first ran these trains would swill with beer in areas other than the buffet, but in later years restrictions were introduced to prevent fans drinking on board.

Recent times have been difficult for travellers, in spite of the motorway system. At least in the '60s there was usually room for you in the ground once you arrived, whether sober or drunk. The spatial restrictions of the smaller stadia of the present mean that there is frequently a lottery system for tickets, and many fans have lost the habit of going week in, week out. The police have taken the job of controlling away fans very seriously – 'herding' is the most usual metaphor. Broadly speaking, away travel has become rather joyless; the province of the fanatics, not the pleasure-seekers.

EDDIE McGRAW My father and my older brothers were Celtic supporters. We didn't get to a great many games because they were miners and they didn't finish until two o'clock; away games were practically impossible to get to. When I left school at 14 and went to the pits, I had pocket money, so I could get to the home games, but very seldom away games, for the same reason – two o'clock finish; you'd to get washed and get away as quick as you could. When I got married I came to Auchenairn. I was in Auchenairn possibly a year, going to Celtic games by public transport, when somebody suggested we try to run a bus to Methil. It was quite successful – we got enough money to pay for it – and we decided we would try to start a club. We looked for people who were prepared to pay beforehand – half a crown for home games in those days. After about three years we had £35 in the bank and we were registered at Celtic Park as a Celtic supporters' club.

We picked up our members on the road to Parkhead – we never ever went in to a pub to get anybody. We didn't think it was right to go inside a pub, then another hundred yards down the road go into another pub, because there were plenty of people on the bus who didn't drink at all. We'd a very good bus. It was very strict.

JIM COOKE They could be quite strict, the buses. In the Coatbridge Rangers Supporters Club we had this Bus Convener, a lad called Alec Meechan. Alec had a lot of friends who met out-with the football, but on a Saturday, Alec was Bus Convener and it was immaterial who his pals were. If they stepped out of line they were off the bus. One night we were on our way home and a lad came away with a remark and he was put off the bus. It was half-past midnight! The poor bloke didn't get back till next morning. Another time we were coming back from Edinburgh and two members started arguing. The argument came to blows, it stopped, one of them started again . . . 'Stop the bus!' They dropped him off by the side of the road. If Alec's granny had been on the bus and she'd stepped out of line, Alec would have put her off.

BILL LAMOND I joined the Dalmarnock Rangers bus, but there were carbon copies of these clubs throughout the Glasgow area, throughout the Lanarkshire area; all the same, with the young team, the middle-aged group and the older men. That all meshed and you got quite a lot of repartee with them all.

JIM COOKE If Rangers went to Dundee, say, the bus left Coatbridge early. At that time we were allowed to take drink on the bus – some of them had cans of beer, some of them had the hard stuff. After the game we went to Keillor's, I think they call the shop, had a meal there; after the meal, some went to one club, some went to another club, some went to the pub; we came back for the bus leaving at 11, half past 11 at night. On the way back quite a few of them had imbibed quite a bit. We'd start singing Rangers songs, we'd start singing Scots songs, and when it got to the wee small hours some of them went back to Sunday School days and they'd give you hymns. In fact the secretary of our club at that time used to go through the Sunday School hymns like no man's business!

EDDIE McGRAW We always left Aberdeen at nine o'clock. We always told them the bus would leave at nine o'clock; they should come at one minute to nine if they wanted it, but not at one minute past because the bus would be away. Coming home in the bus we had very orderly singing. We sang a few rebel songs, but not one of them contained one swear word – we frowned very heavily on that. If you worked in the pit as long as I did you knew a wee bit of French, but we didn't allow it to take over on the bus.

HARVEY BEATON   You could spend the whole weekend at Aberdeen, go up maybe on the Friday night, go to the game on the Saturday and go home on the Sunday; it was the highlight of your calendar. Now you've got motorways it's a lot less friendly. We used to stop off at a place called Auchterarder. They knew we were coming and everybody'd be in for the piano and the sing-song. One time this guy stopped me in Argyle Street – 'How you doing, how you doing?' – and my wife's going, 'Who's that?' And I'm going, 'I know the face . . .' It wasn't until later on that I went, 'That's one of the guys from Auchterarder . . .' The sing-song was terrific.

EDDIE McGRAW   Half-past-two in the morning, we'd get back from Aberdeen. Mary was always waiting on me coming in. I think she was always waiting on her box of chocolates right enough.

On the buses people, as they say, 'made their own entertainment'.

GEORGE MacLEOD   I travelled on quite a few buses, and my father did as well. And when I was travelling, which was probably into the '60s, the entertainment on the buses was just the same as it had been when he'd gone; these buses never changed, really.

JACK JARDINE   I used to leave on a bus that went from the Waverley Pub. You'd have your wee drink, your sing-song, your raffles, your sweeps – every bus had their sweeps. You'd have a lot of blether – who was going to win, the general patter, the discussion of the other team; we were all managers, you know, 'We've got to keep Charlie Fleming out or Gordon Smith, we'll need to get Sammy Cox to get him.' You used to take pieces, flasks – there were no motorways. The whole thing was an occasion, right from morning.

BILL LAMOND   If you went further than Dunfermline you invariably stayed, if not the night, then maybe until one in the morning. That gave everybody time for refreshments. It was a day out going to the game, going to Dundee or Aberdeen or Palmerston in Dumfries. A sweep was one of the things to keep the club funds up – first goal scored and what have you.

EDDIE McGRAW We ran a two-sided raffle – first-half and second-half. Anybody at all who's had any connection with the clubs knows how it works. Celtic goalie, Celtic right-back, Celtic left-back, opposing goalie, opposing right-back, you know . . . first one to score was the winning ticket. Referee first-half, referee second-half, because if there was no score in the first-half the referee won it. All in all you'd have about 50 tickets – you put in some blanks – so you'd raise 50 shillings with that. You gave out 40 and kept ten. That helped to pay the driver.

The Criminal Justice Act that followed the riot at the 1980 Scottish Cup final introduced much tighter regulations about what could be consumed on buses.

JIMMY FINNIS   I still go on the buses every now and then – not so much now because you can't get tickets for some places, and there was a time in the '80s when you were made to feel very unwelcome in towns – treated like cattle and so forth. And then you also had the drink ban – you'd be driving along and the police would stop the bus. It wasn't so innocent as it was when I first started. Then you were kind of out on a spree. Later it was like you were a bother you know, all these signs – 'No Football Coaches'.

FRANK MOOTY They had to take away the drink on the buses; even on our own bus they were well, well on by the time they got to the match. I wasn't a great drinker myself at that time but I could see it happen, quite a few of the boys were causing bother, maybe missing the bus or having to be bailed out.

STEPHEN MURRAY   It definitely means there's less trouble. See when they were drinking on our bus, the 45 minutes from Govan to Parkhead was 45 minutes' drinking time. Now it's 45 minutes' sobering-up time, no matter how much you've had before you get on. It must improve the behaviour in the ground.

ANDY ROBERTSON   When the drink ban came, we had the Chief Inspector of the police on the bus one day. Rangers were playing Hibs at Easter Road. We knew the police were waiting on us getting into Edinburgh; if you'd drink on the bus when you got to Edinburgh you got done. So just before we got to Edinburgh I told everybody to throw their cans and bottles out of the bus. We were just unlucky the way it happened; the police were coming one way and as we passed them everybody flung their cans and bottles out at the same time. So the police turned around on the dual carriageway and stopped us. 'Who's in charge of the bus?' I said 'Eh, me.' 'Right. Where's the drink on the bus?' 'There's nae drink.' 'What was that that yous all just flung oot there?' I said, 'Oh, we had that before we left Larkhall.' 'Who do you think you're taking the piss out of? What's this here?' he said, pointing at the bottle in my dungarees. 'It's a bottle of piss, I was bursting for the toilet.' And he says, 'See if you mention the word piss again, you'll get done, son.' I said, 'It's a bottle of piss.' I drew the bottle out and I gave him it and I said, 'Here, taste it and see.' He just held the bottle and it was like it had just come out a sauna. He turned round and he said, 'You're a spawny bastard,' and flung it out the bus, then went away.

The laughs we've had on the bus, though. We went to Ibrox one day when Rangers played Celtic, and just below the Kingston Bridge the police stopped us, came on and said, 'Are you going to tell all your members up the back to stop hanging out the bus?' I said, 'I'll tell them.' So I said, 'Come on, every one of you, stop hanging out that window. There's no need to hang out that window,' all the rest of it. And then as I was walking back down the bus it just dawned on me, 'The back window doesnae open.' They'd all been banging on the window, singing and that, and the whole window had gone out. We had to walk back from Ibrox that night. The bus company just went off and left us.

FRANK MOOTY   These last few years I've seen change coming; it's been getting stricter with the police; different sorts of things; maybe going to Falkirk or Dundee and the police hounding you, you were maybe parking three miles away from the ground; for years you were parking nearer the park. It's been very, very awkward at times; there must have been different regulations coming in.

Up to the present the buses retain their general character.

COLIN LAMOND The Linwood Supporters Bus – you get a good atmosphere there. Salt of the earth, that's how you would describe the people who go; solid people, people you can trust. People of a quite traditional outlook; people that go to the games regardless of circumstance, no matter how the team's doing; their support for Rangers was passed down from their father and their grandfather and so on. Probably if you got people who went to the rugby at Murrayfield and they got on to one of the supporters' buses from the West of Scotland, maybe Lanarkshire, places like that, they'd probably feel a bit shocked; it wouldn't be the kind of atmosphere that they would feel comfortable in – you know, you're talking about guys – they're no theatre-goers, put it that way – tradesmen and manual workers in traditional industries.

TOMMY HYNDMAN The characters are excellent on our bus, the Celtic Cross bus. Good rapport. Everybody's got a change of name as soon as they get on that bus. Everybody's got a nickname as soon as they join. You've got Fred Flintstone. I'm one of the Dues Brothers. You've got Barney Rubble. There's Fagin – this guy's a publican and he's always rubbing his hands together gleefully, a far-away look in his eyes. One guy, when he's at a game he stands kind of like a totem pole, so he's 'How', he's the Chief. We've got Wilma Flintstone, Perry Como, Yentl . . .

STUART DANIELS We've unbelievable characters on our bus, the Kinning Park Loyal. Laurie Stewart – he's some man, his codename's the Boston Dangler. We've Ron Corleone. Harry Masonic Junior. All Rangers-daft. It's their life. You can shout up the bus to Laurie, 'Is everybody on? Anybody missing?' He'll go, 'Aye, Glenn Miller's missing.' Totally mental. But good camaraderie.

Travellers – whether by buses or by British Rail's Football Specials – seem to be a breed which is, if not extinct, then at least on the endangered species list.

ALAN GALLOWAY   I used to travel. It was magic. You'd go on the Football Specials – you're getting back to the time when I was roundabout 16 to 21 and it was easy to get a ticket. The Football Special always came into Queen Street, because everything's north or east if you're going to away games. It was a great feeling, ending up at parties in Dundee with people you met. I miss that, I miss going to the games now, but because of these lotteries they have now it's the select few who get the tickets for the games they want to go to.

You'd get off the train at Dundee – she's going to kill me when she reads this – and it's the march up to Tannadice Street with your Union Jack draped around your shoulders – proud to be a Rangers supporter – but you're a young boy as well – a couple of cans of beer on the train and it's that kind of, you know – 'Glasgow boys, we are here, we'll shag your women and we'll drink your beer' – and away you all march up with your red, white and blue.

MICK MAHER   I mainly went by bus but sometimes I took the Football Specials. You certainly had a lot of joviality – I remember sleeping in luggage-racks coming back from places. I daresay that if members of the general public – your maiden aunt – had been on the train she might have been quite upset. But the one thing I would say is I never ever witnessed malicious vandalism. The worst act of vandalism I did was one time, coming back from Aberdeen, when we ripped the reserved signs off the train-seats to get ourselves a seat, not realising we were depriving the Queen's Park team who were getting on at Forfar! You'd get a bit of a sing-song as the train started out but it would die out as the journey went on. You'd get good atmosphere, especially if you'd won. But it wasn't wild stuff.

IAIN PATTERSON   In the '70s the 5.30 Glasgow-Stirling-Aberdeen train was packed with Old Firm fans returning from the game. After any Old Firm game the train would be a wall of sound with rival fans singing their heads off. Innocent civilians had to put up with fans banging cans on tables or even jumping on tables as they sang. I think by the late '70s the authorities managed to stop this type of behaviour by banning alcohol on certain trains.

ALAN GALLOWAY   I don't go to away matches now. I object to the lottery at the start of the season. You apply for all your away tickets at the start of the season and basically you take what you get. The first season I was offered Partick Thistle and Dundee United – on a Wednesday night and on some Saturday in January. I want to go to the games but I want to go to the games I want to go to.

BRIAN McBRIDE   It was really the only way that you'd get to see certain parts of Scotland. Most people that live around Glasgow don't travel that much, and to get to Falkirk or parts of Fife or the north, I think you felt that you were at the head of a bunch of gladiators coming to uncivilised places. You really did feel that these were very backward places, that you were the big slickers from Glasgow.

MARK DINGWALL   Travelling? The easiest way to put it is that you're part of an army. When you're going up the motorway or whatever and you're passing cars and buses with Rangers stuff; and you're passing buses that've maybe got pennants of Rangers supporters' clubs in Aberdeen or Manchester or Liverpool; and you're stopping off and people are giving you thumbs-ups and in the villages there's wee groups of kids with Rangers scarves waving at the buses – that definitely makes you feel part of an army. Or a family.

Chapter Six

KINGS of EUROPE
1965–1975

The 1965–75 period was one of great success for Glasgow's clubs; for a period of time their fame as football institutions managed to outstrip their infamy as institutions of quasi-religious bigotry. Of all the many football nights the population has experienced, the European nights of the late '60s and early '70s are the ones Glaswegian supporters remember with most affection. This is partly a matter of an atmosphere – European matches saw grounds packed with home supporters baying as one for the spilling of foreign blood – but also because of the (now lost) standing of Scottish sides in Europe.

It was also a period in which the sight of European footballers was comparatively rare, a case of go to the game or watch the Montford/McPherson highlights. Live European football on television was largely confined to finals, and then only if a British team was involved. The idea of beaming in Italian Serie A matches would have been laughed out of court, and pre-(Rupert) Murdoch there was no option to wire into Sky or Eurosport to pick up highlights of the German Bundesliga or whatever else is the (international) flavour of the day. Fans came to European games as virgins; and the excitement of seeing European games, teams and players – and of course seeing Rangers and Celtic getting wired into them in true Scottish style – was of irresistible proportions.

As well as the big ones – the crucial games on the way to Rangers' and Celtic's winning and losing finals in Lisbon, Nuremberg, Milan and Barcelona – there is a host of less significant matches to remember. The '60s and '70s were times when Old Firm sides would start as favourites against all but the Milans, the Madrids and the Munichs. Poles and Portuguese, for instance, deadly-sounding opposition now for Scots, held no fears; it was a period when qualifying for Europe via the Scottish League meant more than the opportunity to fall before the preliminary-round might of the Champions of Lithuania.

JOHN LARKIN On a European night – I went to an all boys' school – nobody would be concentrating the whole day. Everybody would be geared up; people had their colours on under their uniforms and the place used to go daft – at playtime in the afternoon you'd all be singing.

. . . almost a haze coming off the pitch . . .

TOMMY HYNDMAN The first European night was something special. Before you went in there were the high stairs and you got a chance to see everything – the deep green grass, the floodlights. There was almost a haze coming off the pitch – even the lines were very, very bright, the colours as the teams came out and the roar went up – it still lives with you. On a clear night you'd start seeing the steam and the smoke and all that stuff rising; and it was great to be there.

SANDY STRANG I enjoyed the European nights at Ibrox; I enjoyed one or two at Parkhead too. I've sat at one or two games in the new stand at Ibrox and it was like watching sanitised Subbuteo; it was a more exciting and exhilarating experience being part of a crowd in the '60s. It always rained. One was always soaked to the skin. And it was wonderful. And it wasn't just because you were young and stupid and you didn't know any better; you really felt that you were contributing.

DANNY McGRAIN   On a European night the support might be ninety per cent yours. When you lost a goal there would be silence and you'd actually think, 'It can't be a goal, it must be offside or something.' Then you'd look and see the referee'd given it. It would go quiet for a few seconds. Then the crowd would get behind you and that was you again.

WILLIE JOHNSTON   Abroad you got a lot of spitting – Spaniards, Italians, Greeks. You go down and you think they're picking you up but they're pulling your ear or grabbing your balls. We had one way of keeping cool; we used to just say, 'Glasgow'. We used to love coming out the tunnel at one of those big European games at Ibrox. Now you were talking possibly 80,000 or 85,000 at Ibrox, and as the two teams walked down the tunnel you could actually see the opposition players hearing the noise and going, 'whew'. You knew that they were gone. I mean there were good teams which didn't bottle it, but some – you could see it on their faces.

GEORGE SHERIDAN   You sit nowadays and you watch the likes of Manchester United and Barcelona, these European games in the Champions' League, and you think back – in those days, for a period of five or six years, Celtic were there.

Just before and just after the *annus mirabilis* of 1967, when both Old Firm sides contested a European final, came two violent encounters with English sides. Perhaps the advent of European football brought wider horizons to Scottish football and removed some of the all-or-nothing intensity of Old Firm games; but whatever the allure of the new community of Europe, the old rivalry of Scotland and England died hard. We were in the days when Scottish fans had 'REMEMBER BANNOCKBURN' and '1387' printed on their flags. Celtic–Liverpool and Rangers–Newcastle brought passable imitations of the activities of Robert the Bruce's foot-soldiers.

. . . it was the time of Arthur Montford and his stramashes . . .

JOHN HUGHES   I played at Anfield. We scored a goal and it was a good goal and it would have taken us through, but that's the way it goes. It was the time when the Scottish football programmes would be half made up of English matches; the time of Arthur Montford and his stramashes.

JOHN LARKIN   There was a riot that night. We had arrived and seen the other end but the general response was, 'What's the Kop?' because the Celtic fans that night were unbelievable. You know the Transport and General Workers' banners – they had flags like that, the Celtic fans, with photographs of the faces, maybe John Hughes on one side, on the other side maybe Stevie Chalmers.

Liverpool had this player, Geoff Strong, and nobody marked him because he was limping. Liverpool stuck him on the left wing – there were no substitutes in those days – and somebody fired a ball over and who jumps off one leg to score but this guy Strong? The Kop went mad – it was a lovely sight, I must admit. They scored again. But very near the end Lennox got a through ball and 'scored'; it would have put us through. When they disallowed it the place went mad – they were throwing bottles forward, throwing bottles backward (there were a few Liverpool stragglers, up at the back) – you could have filled a brewery with the bottles they threw that night. Tommy Lawrence, the goal-keeper, was getting further and further back, moving away from the Celtic end; after a bit he was almost at the half-way line and they were still trying to reach him with the bottles – 'Ya bastard!'

WILLIE JOHNSTON   Rangers played Newcastle in a semi-final; maybe '68 or '69; I guess it was the Fairs' Cup. I played down at Newcastle but the only thing I can remember was the fans rioting; the fans coming on the park; a load of young boys, all on the Newkie Brown.

. . . some of our crowd thought English beer was just a lot of rubbish . . .

JIM COOKE   We went to St James's Park. Some of our crowd thought English beer was just a lot of rubbish and they got on to

Newcastle Brown. I've never seen so many bottles – empty bottles, of course – flying in my life as I did that night. The Rangers fans were at one end, Newcastle at the other. A crowd of yobboes from the Newcastle support jumped over the wall and they came up *en masse* to taunt the Rangers supporters. Of course you don't do that if you've any sense.

In 1967 Rangers played their second European final and Celtic their first. For Celtic, Lisbon, where they faced Inter Milan, became a place of immortal memory; Rangers met Bayern Munich in Nuremberg which they found – well, a bit of a trial.

TOMMY HYNDMAN   1967. The year that Celtic won everything, including the Eurovision Song Contest.

DAVID POTTER   I was at St Andrews University during the Lisbon season, so I didn't see any of those games in the flesh. I followed them avidly on the radio. I remember being laughed at round about the turn of that year; I put a pound on Celtic to win that European Cup. I must have been drunk at the time. They beat Zurich, then a French side, FC Nantes. The Vojvodina game – the quarter-final – I remember watching without knowing the score. Arthur Montford introduced it and told us it was a cliffhanger . . .

CHARLIE GALLAGHER   They reckoned our name was on the Cup when we came through that one. In the last minute I took the famous corner-kick. When I used to meet somebody, a stranger, they'd say, 'Oh, Charlie, I remember that corner-kick . . .' and I'd say, 'Oh, do you?' and they'd say, 'Yes, I was standing right behind you.' Everybody I talked to was standing right behind me. I always figured there must have been a big, big queue of people all the way from Celtic Park to Hampden – because if you listened to these stories then nobody stood anywhere else.

DAVID POTTER   The semi-final against Dukla Prague was very tense because, having won at home, they played defensively away. It was perhaps the first time that Celtic had done that. I think they put the last 20 minutes on Radio Scotland live. Dukla were pressing all that time. I remember at one point walking across the floor and the commentator thought they'd scored – it went just over the bar – and my legs just went under me.

NEIL McDERMOTT   There was a feeling that we were going all the way. There was the song – 'We're on our way to Lisbon, we shall not be moved' – and as the season went on what started off as faith and hope became more of a conviction. Having said that when they reached the final and they had to play Inter Milan – maybe I'm a defeatist, a pessimist – I didn't think they could do it.

I've selt the hoose . . . I want to go to Lisbon . . .

HUGH FERRIE   One story I heard was about a man in Maryhill who came in and said to his wife, 'I've selt the hoose.' She said, 'What?' 'I want to go to Lisbon,' he says, 'I had to get the money. You can go and live with your maw.' Guys were hiring kilts all over the place. Didn't even fit them. They looked ridiculous. A colleague went to Lisbon, or maybe he went to the airport to see some people off. He said that some of the planes that had been chartered could hardly get off the ground. People were praying as they were taking off.

MICK MAHER   My uncle ran a bus to Lisbon from Muirhill. I had an uncle Eddie who lived in the south of France; and they said, right, we can stay there for the night. They arrived there late and of course they didn't really know his address. My uncle Eddie told me later that he thought they must have been delayed. Just as he was going to bed he heard – in the middle of this quiet French street – 'Oh it's a grand old team . . .' They'd been walking up and down and not finding anywhere, so they just stood there and sang Celtic songs till someone came out.

HUGH TONER   I think I'd to buy a scarf specially for Lisbon. I took my son Brian – he was just eight and was wearing a special jumper that had been knitted for him. He'd seen every round of the Cup – he was a sort of mascot. The joiners in my work – they were all Rangers supporters – made him a big rickety rattle done up in green, white and gold. This thing was monstrous.

Every time the bus went round the corner all you could hear was bottles rolling from one side to the other . . .

JOHN LARKIN I set off wearing a suit and a tie, just holding a flag. I had a scarf; I've still got it, it's about 31 years old – d'you remember those scarves? They had the white tassels, like dress scarves.

The plan was that we would leave from The Old Farmhouse about ten o'clock – I think the pubs closed at ten o'clock in those days. So we set off, and I thought, we'll get down to the coast. Well, after about 20 or 30 miles the first guy says 'I need the toilet', and they all jump out. We go on another half hour, another 20 or 30 miles, same thing. Every time the bus went round a corner all you could hear was bottles rolling from one side to the other. It was like that all the way from Glasgow to Bayonne, the 'first stop'.

The kick off was at 5.20 on the Thursday and I think we finally got to Lisbon at a quarter to five. We just parked in this big square and jumped in a taxi. The taxi-driver took my flag and he had it out the window. The place was going daft, it really was; there were so many people wearing green and white. They were Sporting Lisbon fans – you'd go up to them and you'd think they were Celtic fans; half of Lisbon was in green and white.

ADAM SHIELS I set off on the Monday night from a pub in Hamilton called the Moy Bar. When we got through into Spain, there were rumours going through the bus that we'd taken the wrong route. We ended up in Madrid, and that was where the fun started – because we realised we weren't going to get to Lisbon on time. There was a plane going. Me and two of my pals were sitting in the bus nearly in tears. The next thing one of the women from the desk had come up and said there were still seven or eight seats left up the front of the plane, so that was panic stations. We still couldn't really afford it; but we said, we've come this far, we're going all the way, we don't care if we've to eat grass. I just gave them everything, there's the cheque-book, everything, take whatever you want!

. . . the Italian team looked at us as if to say, 'Who the hell's this we're playing today?'

TOMMY GEMMELL Inter Milan were the favourites; we were the also-rans, a wee team called Celtic from Scotland. I think this worked in our favour. Coming out the tunnel Bertie Auld – his usual flamboyant self – started singing 'The Celtic Song' and we all chipped in. The Italian team who were coming out alongside us looked at us as if to say, 'Who the hell's this we're playing today?'

BILLY McNEILL 1967 was easy for us in a sense that we were the underdogs, and outside of our own country very few people would ever have given us a chance. But we had an attitude that we used to think and believe that on the day we could beat anyone. We had another great break that day, because they got a penalty kick very early in the game, which gave us this feeling of injustice.

DAVID POTTER The final was built up in a way that Jim Craig would call gallus – it was on both BBC and STV. Arthur Montford said something about, 'Oh, you may have gathered there's a football match on tomorrow.'

It was the day before my first year Greek exams. I remember booking my seat in my residence hall, a seat near the TV. I sat there all afternoon with a copy of Homer's *Iliad Book I* and Homer's *Iliad Book IX* on my lap. Everyone was getting very excited. And then the television in our hall broke down seconds before Inter Milan's penalty so all we heard was the sound telling us that Inter had scored. We rushed up the road – I was in tears – to another hall. As I ran up there there was nobody around. Just nobody around. It was like the aftermath of a nuclear bomb or something. Everybody was in front of the television, even in St Andrews, which is not exactly a hotbed of Scottish football.

ADAM SHIELS   The Celtic crowd were stunned at first but I'd say there must have been close on 18,000 Celtic supporters there, and a lot of the Portuguese were shouting on the Celtic too. The Celtic supporters all moved down to the end where the goals were scored. As the game went on and on, we thought, 'Is it never going to come?' You felt it was coming, but at the same time, no – hitting the bar, Sarti making some tremendous saves. Big Gemmell had tried the same move five times and not got anywhere; the next thing he got the goal and you've never felt so much relief in your life.

EDDIE McGRAW   I would say when Gemmell scored the goal we jumped five feet in the air. A jump off the bum, not the feet, just with pure bum-muscle. Right up.

MARGARET DEVLIN   I wasn't there in body; I was there in spirit, let me tell you. Mary-Jo was six weeks old at the time. Here I was, feeding Mary-Jo, and Celtic scored; and Mary-Jo went up into the air. Gerry was through in Dalkeith watching it. He stayed with an elderly couple who had gone out to church in the evening. He had to sit and watch the game on his own. That must have been dreadful! He said Celtic scored and he jumped up and he shouted, 'Oh, yes! Ya beauty!' And he looked around the room. And there was no one there.

BRIAN McBRIDE   Everyone in Glasgow remembers what they were doing that day. I was 11 at the time and it was the first time I'd really watched a match on television with things like action replays. And I do remember when Tommy Gemmell equalised and they showed the replay I thought they'd scored a second goal of the exact same type.

TOMMY GEMMELL   Still – if that move had broken down and Inter had broken away and scored a goal I would have got my backside kicked. Jim Craig had overlapped on the right-hand side and here was he squaring the ball to me just outside the box

– the Italian defender hesitated and turned back and I scored. If that had been blocked I was the one who was going to get a bollocking because I shouldn't have been up there if Jim Craig was up.

JIMMY FINNIS All I remember about seeing the winner go in was pandemonium – I was in a mate's house; we were packed in; and, I'm not sure, but I think the commentator makes a mistake and he thinks Lennox has scored, or Murdoch – and it was Stevie Chalmers. And I remember the whole room buzzing with these different names – who's got it? Who's got it? I'm not the biggest guy in the world and I was leaping up and down trying to get a look over somebody's shoulders.

NEIL McDERMOTT It's the only football match my wife has ever watched in its entirety. In fact she's one up on me – I missed the last five minutes. I couldn't bear to watch. I was in another room. We had an English commentator, Kenneth Wolstenholme. Jock Stein used to laugh afterwards that Kenneth Wolstenholme came up to him afterwards and said, 'We've done it!' He'd become one of us.

. . . I was doing a headstand, I remember, and someone recognised me . . .

JOHN LARKIN About ten minutes before the final whistle, the end where Celtic had scored was just packed with people. There was a moat, no water in it, but it was quite a jump; and the police were all standing on the other side. At the final whistle we all jumped this moat; they stopped a few, then they gave up. On the pitch I met people I hadn't seen for years. I was doing a headstand, I remember, and someone recognised me.

BILLY McNEILL I don't have any vivid and sharp pictures of the final whistle at all; my memory isn't all that clear until after I had been presented with the trophy, on my own. By the time I'd got back to the dressing-room I'd lost the Inter Milan shirt I'd exchanged my own jersey for; I'd lost a pair of boots.

Everybody lost something that day. It was quite funny; going back in that day on the bus we passed a car with a whole lot of Portuguese in it and there were about three of them waving boots and stockings out the window.

CHARLIE GALLAGHER After the game? I'll not tell you some of the stories . . . there were some magnificent things done that night!

SEAN FALLON All the boys let their hair down and enjoyed themselves, that's all I'll say. And the supporters – they were more elated than the players.

ADAM SHIELS It was tremendous. I can actually mind saying – kneeling down on the grass – 'I don't care if I die here, I can go any time now'. But when we came out and the reality hit us – what are we going to do, we've no money – it's next Tuesday before we get home and we've no money. One fellow – an older man – actually bought me some food, a bag of chips here and there. All the supporters looked out for each other.

JOHN LARKIN The next day we were setting off for home. Just as we were leaving, we heard this bus in the distance, with all banging on the sides, 'Hail, Hail, the Celts are here . . .' We went, 'What the hell's this?' And the guys on this bus, they all say, 'What was it like? What was it like?' They said they'd got lost in Spain, realised they weren't going to make it and watched it on television in Madrid.

EDDIE McGRAW The players came in to the airport. Bob Rooney had his arms round about the top of two women – he was blotto. Big Yogi, his tie was way over to here. Bertie Auld came in with Joe McBride and he got mobbed. And Bertie – wait a minute, wait a minute – 'Oh it's a grand old team' – they had them singing, you see? But the smartest man – absolutely immaculate, the wife on his arm – was Steve Chalmers.

JACK PRIOR Portugal was brilliant. They kept the cafés open all night and we were singing all night and nobody bothered us – it was the greatest night in the world.

In the morning when we woke up none of us knew where our hotels were, so we just made our way to the airport. We'd missed our planes and everything, but they soon got rid of us all, gradually, phoning through, asking us where did we come from, what was our number, what plane should we have been on; the whole airport was full of these people – did they know where they were going? Did they hell. Half of them didn't even come by plane; half of them maybe came by bus but ended up going back on the plane; and half of them didn't know where they were.

In Glasgow? I was supposed to go to work the next day, but I didn't even get to work – I was too busy trying to get to the pub to give the big roars and that; we were there, we'd done it.

MICK MAHER I had actually to fly back to sit my Higher Spanish exam. I think it's Andy Warhol said something about how everybody gets their 15 minutes of fame. We left Lisbon at maybe midnight; went home and had a few hours sleep then got up and went to school. Everyone was up at the window, cheering; at lunchtime everyone wanted to speak to you and shake your hand; you were there.

There was a boy called Mick Boyle who's in Canada now and he said, 'We all think you're lucky, because we all watched it on television, but you'll be able to tell your grandchildren – I was there . . .'

Needless to say, I told my children and they said, 'Well that was a long, long time ago . . .'

. . . back on to working 12-hour shifts . . .

ADAM SHIELS At that time, I was actually working in the steelworks – I'd just turned 18. I'd got a fortnight off of my work to go to Lisbon. The day I came back, I arrived back from Lisbon on a Tuesday, and I phoned on the Wednesday morning and told the manager I was back home and asked when would they like me to start? – thinking that was me till the following

Monday. Six o'clock on Wednesday night. Back on to working 12-hour shifts.

ALEX BELL As a Rangers fan in London I wanted Celtic to win the European Cup. I wanted a Scottish team to win it before an English team.

COLIN GLASS I wanted Celtic to win the European Cup when they went in against Inter Milan. I thought it would be a victory for attacking football. But by the time they got to the next final in 1970, I was fed up hearing about it. Looking at it now I can see that both their goals in Lisbon were offside. According to my video recorder they are, anyway.

BILL LAMOND It's true to say that at the time when Celtic played Dukla in the European Cup and beat them, they were applauded on to the park by the Rangers team of that time; the Rangers stood and made a guard of honour. But I should think they were about the only Rangers people that were behind the Celtic. I'm not biased; it was a terrific achievement. But I certainly would rather have seen Inter Milan win. I think ninety-five per cent of Rangers supporters were the same. And had the boot been on the other foot I'm sure you'd have got the same story. It didn't bring the city together. It'd take more to bring them together.

JOHN GREIG I think I wanted Celtic to win the European Cup. I think that the city of Glasgow came very, very close to a magnificent achievement, with two clubs winning the two major European competitions that year. We – the two clubs together – were a whisker away from creating a record that would probably never be achieved again.

The distance of a 'whisker' was the narrow defeat Rangers suffered in their second European final. This time it was the Cup Winners' Cup.

GEORGE MacLEOD The run-up to Rangers' Nuremberg final against Bayern Munich was strange because there were some close calls; Dortmund was close, and then we beat Real Zaragoza – was it on away goals? There weren't penalties, anyway – maybe it was a toss of the coin or drawing lots. Whatever they did at that time. And the semi-final was tight, against Slavia Sofia.

ALEC WILLOUGHBY We probably had one of our finest results over in Bulgaria. We had so many injuries and had to play a side that had seven Bulgarian internationalists. Davie Wilson and I put together wouldn't make much more than six foot, but the two of us kept four guys of six foot, six foot two occupied for 90 minutes. You don't get any pats on the back for that – but we knew the job we'd done.

SANDRA LEWSEY The thing was we had matched Celtic all the way, round for round; and they had won it the week before, and it was 'Let's do a double for Scotland' sort of thing.

WILLIE JOHNSTON By the time we played in Nuremberg the season had been finished for two or three weeks. We were playing friendlies – we played Morton at Cappielow, we played Motherwell at Fir Park and we still had ten days before the final. We actually went to Canada and played a game in Toronto just to keep playing. Dukla Prague or somebody.

. . . they all knew what shops to go in to nick stuff . . .

CHARLIE LOGAN I went to Nuremberg with a bar in Brigton, the Mermaid. I was only a kid . . . 18. It was murder. I was down at Brigton Cross paying the money for the ticket maybe on the Saturday and Celtic were back in town with the European Cup.

Some of the men on the bus had travelled before – at least they all knew what shops to go in to nick stuff. In those days there wasn't your toilet on the bus – it was the bottle or bucket down at the front; the bus didn't stop because you were hammering on. You would stand at the door and pee in this bucket, right? We wouldn't stop to chuck it off, even; we'd just open the door and pour it out. And this guy fell out of the door onto the road! We looked back and all we could see were all these headlights behind us and this guy lying in the middle of a

German motorway at two o'clock in the morning. We didn't go back for him; we heard he got a fractured skull or something but he was all right.

The guys from the Mermaid were not exactly what you would call gentlemen. On the way back they had a carry out at the back of the bus and they took one of these wee barrels of beer and stuck it in the back of the last two seats, sort of wedged it there; they went to open it and it exploded. It went skooshing right down the middle of the bus – everyone was knee deep in froth. There were loads of fights before the game as well in the station bar – chairs were flying back and forth – it was something to do with a slight language difficulty . . .

ALEC WILLOUGHBY I was left out of the Nuremberg side; Roger Hynd played instead. I actually went and asked Symon why I'd been left out. Symon had signed me as a schoolboy and I had a lot to be grateful to him for, but he wasn't the kind to explain; he belonged to the 'I pick the team and you have no right to know why' era. So I never found out why.

WILLIE JOHNSTON Celtic had Jock Stein; Rangers had Scot Symon. When we played Bayern Munich we were so disorganised it wasn't true. They had Beckenbauer, Muller, Roth and everyone playing – and we got beat 1–0 in extra-time. That was a sickener.

COLIN GLASS They screwed it up in Nuremberg. Playing a man like Roger Hynd at centre-forward. I still remember seeing that on TV. There was one occasion where he just seemed to need to almost blow the ball in with his head, and the goalkeeper was stranded, on the ground, couldn't get up, and Roger Hynd just needed to touch it with his head. He leaped up and bulleted the header, you know, the way a player is taught to header, right down into the ground; and it bounced up into the keeper's arms. By doing the difficult thing, he screwed it up.

JOHN GREIG We played a lot of great sides and I think probably we were just unfortunate in getting Bayern Munich in Nuremberg with a big home support. I'm not making excuses.

Some people say we played harder sides than Celtic had to to win their Cup, but I appreciate how hard it was for Celtic to win their games. I mean the opposition may look stronger or weaker on paper but it doesn't always happen that way when you cross the white line to play against them.

. . . a wee bit of conscience, maybe . . .

ALEC WILLOUGHBY When I came back from my travels many, many years later – South Africa, Australia, Hong Kong – Scot Symon was General Manager of Partick Thistle. I got a call at my mother's one day to say he'd seen me in Glasgow and would I take a wee run up? The manager of Partick at that time was Bertie Auld, the Lisbon Lion; and Bertie, being a Glasgow guy, says, 'I know you're not up here to see me, Willoughby,' and I says, 'Aye, you're right.' So I went in and Symon and I had a cup of tea and a blether. I must have been there a good couple of hours and Nuremberg was never mentioned . . . but I don't know whether he wanted me to see that, incidentally, Alec, he knew he'd made a mistake that day. A wee bit of conscience, maybe.

Any inclination to call Nuremberg a disaster disappeared after the sombre events of the afternoon of 2 January 1971, when 66 people died, trampled or crushed as they left Ibrox. Likewise, casual use of the word 'tragedy' to describe an own goal or an away defeat in Europe disappeared. The victims are memorialised by the magnificence of the new Ibrox, the foundation-stones of which were laid not as a result of the Taylor Report, but as a result of what happened on Stairway 13 that grim afternoon.

. . . I automatically said, 'They didn't beat us, did they?'

SANDRA LEWSEY I wasn't at the game. I think I'd just got engaged or something stupid like that – you know how you do these things. I always remember we went home, up to my dad's and my dad said, 'Did you hear about the disaster up at Ibrox? I automatically said, 'Oh no. They didn't beat us did they?'

HUGH FERRIE My daughter Audrey used to go to the games with me. We left early, and as we came out we heard this tremendous roar – Rangers had equalised. And just at that point people were coming down this big stairway and some ran up to see what was happening, others were coming down. One or two fell and they went down like dominoes. Sixty-six people died.

ADAM SHIELS The police just actually put rows and rows of bodies on the football park; is that not a sight to sadden everybody? Sixty-six people killed because of a goal.

JACK JARDINE I remember something happened at the top and we all turned. I was with Archie McArthur at the top and then I lost him. I saw an old guy – I can remember that old guy to this day burling away down the hill, rolling down the steep hill, you know. I still don't know what happened to him.

ALEX MILLER That day I got left out of the team. Willie Mathieson came back from injury, so I never played. But, thinking I was playing, I had sold ten tickets to friends of mine. Three of the ten lost their lives. One of them was my juvenile team manager, who had stayed in my house the night before.

. . . you just thought, the neds at the top of the hill probably having a go at each other . . .

JACK PRIOR As far as I was concerned the game was a draw and that was all it was. I went away from the ground, saw a few ambulances, but you never thought – you just thought, the neds at the top of the hill probably having a go at each other, they've probably come out the one door and run into each other. We went down the road and I did a pub crawl with a couple of the boys; and everybody's out on the street and they're phoning here and phoning there, looking for me, they thought I was under the stampede. As I say, I had two or three halfs in each pub all the way down, ending up at our own pub: 'Everyone's been phoning, and your ma's on the phone and your cousin's down driving around in cars . . .' And I'm going, 'What's wrang?' I had to phone the auld wife and she was greeting, so I had to just get up the road and see the old dutch.

ANDY ROBERTSON Two of my mates got killed; big Jim Gray and Jim Mair. I was from here to you with them. We went to the game as usual, New Year's Day, you're getting a right good drink and that. When Colin Stein scored me and my mates were walking out, and honest to God, our feet weren't touching the ground. We got onto the stairs, and there was nothing to stop you; you had 10,000 people behind you, shoving you down the steep stairs. You didn't know it had happened, because you were just away; you couldn't get back into the ground; we knew there was something wrong because there was ambulance, ambulance, ambulance, going up and back all the time, but it was all cordoned off. Big Jim Gray and Jim Mair; and the only reason they could tell it was Jim Mair was because of the tattoos and his teeth. They couldn't tell his face; it was all trampled.

SANDRA LEWSEY You couldn't describe what you felt – you felt that these 66 people were your family. It was so hard to come to terms with. You could picture exactly what had happened – these huge big terraces, they were absolutely massive – and you just knew exactly where these people had been, you knew exactly what had happened, and although you weren't there you were there. It was just an absolute nightmare.

DAVID POTTER I went to see someone in Polmont, between Glasgow and Edinburgh. I remember getting on the train, and there were people there who knew something about it, but no one knew how bad it was. The atmosphere was very quiet – both Celtic and Rangers supporters were there, very quiet, and one fellow was actually crying – a Rangers supporter crying on the shoulder of a Celtic supporter. Everybody else was quiet.

STEF JARDINE Maybe we should have seen it coming, because my memories of going to Ibrox when I was a wee guy were of running down the hill. Nobody used the stairs because the stairs were that congested. It was that steep too, you'd start off dead steady and you'd end up going down at 200 miles an hour.

ADAM SHIELS Just to think about it was terrible, because I had been in big crowds. I went to Paisley one time, and the game was ready to start and there were thousands outside and I was crushed, against a lamp-post in fact, and I thought, if I go down now I'm away. A couple of the older men round about actually got me and passed me right over the crowd. And that was only what you'd term a wee game, a Celtic–St Mirren. From that you could imagine what it must have been like if you lost your footing at Ibrox. I've seen it happen coming out of Hampden, coming down the old stairs they had at the time. If people maybe stood on the back of your shoes, you couldn't just stop, you had to keep going, maybe go back to look 20 minutes later.

SANDRA LEWSEY The next game after the disaster was awful. You wanted to go but you didn't want to be there. And when you were there you just couldn't concentrate. I can't even remember who we played. To be honest I don't even remember the game. I just remember the atmosphere was – very sad.

NEIL McDERMOTT At the time it seemed like it might do some good – if you can have any good come out of that. There were masses offered in all the churches for the victims; it was all Rangers supporters, every one, who died – and Celtic players attended services and so on along with the Rangers ones – and it seemed as if people had learned there were more important things in life than a football match. But it didn't last – in a game or two they were back to the usual hatred.

DAVID PALMER That was a tragic day for the whole of Glasgow and the whole of football. Scottish and English football, because of the traditions of keeping themselves separate, have tended not to talk to each other and I've always felt that if English football had been more aware of New Year 1971 then possibly Hillsborough might not have happened.

With all the Euroexcitement, it might be forgotten – though not by their fans – that Celtic were building an eminent list of successive Championship successes. For some, memories of the run are a bit vague; for Rangers fans memories of the end of the run – in the last year of the old First Division – are most precise.

TOMMY GEMMELL The 1967 one is the only one that really sticks out. We went to Ibrox for the second last game of the season. They had to beat us to be in with any kind of a chance and Herrera was over to watch us from Inter Milan. We drew 2–2 and Jimmy Johnstone scored a goal from the corner of the box with his left foot; it had never been known and was never repeated. It was pissing down with rain – really heavy conditions; and it left us with nothing on our minds except the Scottish Cup final, the European Cup final and a wee event at Wembley when we beat the English team for the first time since the World Cup.

CHARLIE GALLAGHER I played in some of the early Championships of the nine-in-a-row; '65–'66, '66–'67, '67–'68 – I got a medal for each of those. I had a good year in '67–'68 – that was my best year. 1967–'68 does stick in my mind because there's been a few books written about it and they refer to it as Gallagher's Campaign. There was a spell at Celtic Park when I played for three seasons and I wasn't in a losing team.

TONY GRIFFIN One recollection is of the League Cup final of 1966. Before the match started, the Rangers support took advantage of the westerly wind to send bunches of red, white, blue and orange balloons bouncing down the ground towards the Celtic End. All were blown off course or burst when they reached the terracing, except for one solitary blue balloon that trundled towards the Celtic goal. As the Rangers support became aware of its progress, a roar went up at the Mount Florida end, but at the last moment a young boy of 12 or 13 dashed out from the Celtic support, dodged the 'polis' who had come to intercept him and gleefully booted the ball off the goal-line, out for a 'corner', to a tumultuous roar from the King's Park end! Uncannily, the cameo was repeated for real during the game itself. With Celtic leading 1–0 and Rangers attacking furiously, Alex Smith ran onto a through ball from John Greig, stumbled but still managed to prod the ball past the diving keeper. It looked a certain goal, but Willie O'Neil raced the ball to the line and kicked it clear – a save that won the Cup for Celtic.

It was the night The Fugitive *was ending on TV . . . the bookies were even offering odds on whodunit . . .*

EUGENE MacBRIDE The night I will always remember was in 1967. Celtic had just won the European Cup and they played Rangers in the League Cup. Rangers scored in eight minutes and held that lead right through the first half and into the second half. Then they were awarded a penalty and it looked like curtains – but Johansen hit the bar. And as it rebounded he hit it himself, you see – free-kick to Celtic, and they went straight up the park and Wallace scored. And they scored again a minute or two later, I think Bobby Murdoch. And we were in the stand. And in the stand, suddenly, the feet began to stamp. There was Celtic triumphalism. And a third goal went in. It was the night *The Fugitive* was ending on TV and everybody was wondering what the ending was going to be – the bookies were even offering odds on whodunit. My father and I left Parkhead and we walked all the way down to Argyle Street – one of our marathons – and I remember saying to him, 'Changed days' – and my father, who never had very much to say – he said, 'Changed days, aye.'

DAVIE HAY After a few years you started to forget; you couldn't tell one Championship from the other. You seem to remember having paraded the League Championship, but you're always confused; that run round Easter Road, was that the seventh one or the eighth one? You become blasé about it.

DENIS CONNAGHAN The number 'nine' in a row did matter; every year past six, which was a British record, mattered; then it became common knowledge that MTK Budapest had done it nine times in a row so that was what we were after. Every year they brought out a new tie, with a seven, eight, nine emblem.

JOHN WATSON   Did Rangers fans feel the pain of the nine-in-a-row? I felt it. My dad used to come back every Saturday and boot my backside in!

. . . I came out the Gorbals with a Salman Rushdie mask on . . .

STUART DANIELS   The whole thing was a downer. I stayed in the Gorbals for over 20 years. I came through the terrible nine-in-a-row by you know who. In fact, I came out the Gorbals with a Salman Rushdie mask on.

Derek Johnstone played 'The Sash' on the moothie . . .

COLIN GLASS   I can remember the date it ended exactly – 11th of January 1975. Up to New Year Celtic had been leading the League until we played them at New Year. We beat them 3–0 at Ibrox; we destroyed them and their confidence. The following week Rangers were at Dumbarton and Celtic were playing Motherwell at Parkhead. Rangers won 5–1 – I think Tommy McLean got a hat-trick – and Celtic went down 3–2. Willie Pettigrew – remember him? – scored for Motherwell. That night we got the 6.10 train back to Dundee from Glasgow Queen Street and Derek Johnstone was on the train. There were Rangers and Celtic fans on the train and we were taunting them quite ruthlessly, asking them if their mother was well, quite infantile really. Then somebody got out a mouth organ and we started singing, and Derek Johnstone played 'The Sash' on the moothie – there was no trouble, no fighting, just a good party.

However, just as Celtic had in the bad times of the '50s, Rangers had some joy in the cups during this period. As then, scarcity of success makes for good memories, with victories savoured.

ALEC WILLOUGHBY   In '65-'66 the Cup final day was a Saturday and at that particular time what Celtic were going to do to Rangers was nobody's business; and it finished up that Scot Symon picked a team on the basis that – well, we may not win but we're certainly not going to get beat. He drafted in a wing-half called Bobby Watson and though the wing-half would normally wear the number 4 jersey he gave him the number 8 jersey that that season belonged to myself. It was 0–0 on the Saturday but it was a moral victory for Rangers. On the Wednesday Johansen scored the one that sometimes you can only score in a Cup final.

. . . one of my pals went out for a pie at quarter past two and couldn't get back in again . . .

COLIN GLASS The best football match I've ever seen was the 1973 Scottish Cup final. Celtic had a really good side that season. They won the League, just, from us. We won 26 games from the January, but we'd got off to a bad start. At that Cup final, there were 40,000 people in the Rangers End and the official attendance was 120,000, and I know there was a break-in at the Rangers End that day. One of my pals went out for a pie at quarter past two and couldn't get back in again.

John Greig had a tremendous save in that game. In those days you weren't sent off for doing that. He wasn't the most agile but he leaped across the goal with McCloy beaten. And I remember in that game Derek Johnstone playing keepie-uppie in the six-yard box surrounded by three Celtic players. Talk about keeping your cool in an absolute cauldron – it was an astonishing piece of bravado and skill. Totally gallus.

When that happened we were totally high – there isn't a drug on earth that can give the feeling we had. And the support – long after five o'clock the whole of the north enclosure was just a sea of blue and white scarves.

JIMMY BROWN My favourite Rangers–Celtic game must be the time when we won the Cup 3–2 in the final at Hampden; 1973 was it? When Derek Johnstone headed against one post, it ran along, hit the other post, and Tom Forsyth, with his studs, from nine inches, managed to get the ball just over the line and no more! I still wake up in the middle of the night and think he's going to miss it.

Another reason why '60s football is held in high esteem is that the wingers were still around; Jimmy Johnstone and Willie Henderson, two wee number 7s, provided a tuneful swansong for the art of old-fashioned Scottish wing-play.

SANDY STRANG I remember this match in the early '70s where Henderson and Johnston played; these enormous bales of straw were used to cover the pitch, and of course the New Year's Day game, the great revenue spinner, just had to go ahead, and these enormous bales of straw were in the corners.

The game developed into a battle between Greig and Gemmell, who were the respective right-backs, and the two number 7s; Greig and Gemmell were kicking Johnstone and Henderson respectively. Eventually Greig hammered Johnstone, such that he bounced into the straw, and I remember him climbing out with this sheepish expression, straw in his ginger thatch, looking rather like the farmer's boy who'd been discovered in the loft with the farmer's favourite daughter. And I remember the Rangers fans at that end breaking into song, singing 'Molly Malone', with the concluding line being, 'As she wheeled her wheelbarrow,/ Through streets broad and narrow,/ Crying . . .' And here they burst into clapping, and sang, 'Gemmell's a bastard!' And Gemmell – I was in the enclosure only ten yards away from him – was laughing and smiling like an orchestra conductor waving this pretend baton. Meanwhile, Greig was sharpening his boot at the other end.

JOHN GREIG The 'bales of straw game' was before under-soil heating came into effect. It was really bad weather at that time around New Year's and to protect the pitch Celtic had covered it in bales of straw. Because they did that the ground was very slippy. I accidentally bumped into wee Jimmy a few times that day and he ended up in the straw. The laugh is that as we went off at half time he had straw sticking out his head – he looked like Wurzel Gummidge.

Because of the nine-in-a-row Championship run, Celtic had several cracks at regaining their European Cup. They came closest to a repetition of 1967 in 1970. By winning their Auld Enemy semi-final against Don Revie's great Leeds United side they had one hand on the Cup. Feyenoord's docker support had other ideas.

. . . A fan wanted to know the draw and I said 'Leeds' and he went, 'Oh, no' . . .

BILLY McNEILL The last four were ourselves, Leeds, Feyenoord and one of the Eastern European teams, was it Legia Warsaw? I remember when the draw was made picking up the phone at Celtic Park; a fan wanted to know the draw and I said, 'Leeds', and he went 'Oh, no.'

NEIL McDERMOTT I was at the Leeds game – the highest crowd for a European match – it'll probably go down in history as that. 134,000 – a seething mass of humanity – partly for Leeds – the superteam of the time and an English team – but partly because a lot of people had dismissed Celtic.

. . . you ever see someone blushing on black-and-white telly? . . .

HUGH TONER Celtic had won 1–0 in Leeds. At Hampden, when Leeds equalised – that didn't matter. Jimmy Johnstone was unstoppable that night. At one point it went quiet, and you could hear voices from the park, you know, when you're in the stand. And Jackie Charlton says to Norman Hunter, 'Take him, go for him . . .' And Hunter shouts back, 'You do it!' Johnstone's running up to Hunter and Hunter, going backwards, just falls over. He was going backwards that fast he fell on his backside. It was priceless.

You ever see someone blushing on black-and-white telly? Well, David Coleman was talking to Stein and he said, 'Tonight, people now know how good a team you are, you've proved how good a team you are.' 'No,' Stein says, 'We didn't need this to show how good a team this is. You ask Shankly, Matt Busby – all these people knew we were a good team. Only English commentators didn't realise how good a team we were. People who knew about football knew we were a good team.'

JOHN LARKIN What I always remember was Billy Bremner and Eddie Gray, who were Celtic fans, going up to the fans at the end. They'd lost the game but they were probably not that disappointed.

I went up by train. I was wearing a new jacket – a sort of jerkin thing. I came back with half the sleeve off my jacket, and only one shoe. I lost that when we equalised – you couldn't put your feet on the ground, it was unbelievable. I felt so proud to go back to work. Before, I was so nervous, as if I was playing myself. Because, living in England, if you were a Celtic fan, you were on a hiding to nothing, nobody took Scottish football seriously. And I remember going back to work and I thought, stuff you lot, we've done it, we're in the final again. In Milan.

GEORGE SHERIDAN Milan – if there was an example of hell on earth, that was it.

JOHN LARKIN I think in Lisbon there were about twelve thousand, and I think because people had missed the glory of that time, there were about twenty-five thousand who went to Milan. We thought it was going to be the same, we thought we would outnumber the Feyenoord supporters, that they would all be 'ho-de-ho-de-ho-de-ho,' and all that. Then we saw them – they were absolutely massive – they were all dockers. It was the first time I'd ever seen an organised support, like somebody was conducting them – they were swaying the whole game, blowing horns. They were so colourful – it was the best support I'd ever seen.

. . . It was like Scotland–Peru in Argentina . . .

JIMMY FINNIS Gemmell scored and everything was going okay – it was like Scotland–Peru in Argentina, cruising – and everything started to go wrong. They equalised. Then worse.

114

JOHN HUGHES I missed a good chance in the game that maybe would have won us it. Stein blamed the players afterwards, but he gave the players complacency, and he realised too late. The attitude in the dressing-room was that we only had to turn up to win.

TOMMY GEMMELL We got the impression that we were playing a side from the lower reaches of the Scottish First Division. An example – Stein said there was a guy on the left side of midfield that was like Jim Baxter; that after half-time we wouldn't see him. And the guy's name was Van Hanegem; he went on to get over a hundred caps for Holland and he controlled the game from start to finish.

GEORGE SHERIDAN The game itself was absolutely terrible – I think a lot of people were feeling, when it was 1–1, 'Oh, for God's sake somebody score, even if it's them' – because to spend another two days, waiting for a replay – it would have been better to lose.

MICK MAHER I still wake up in the night hearing those Feyenoord horns. I can remember it vividly but for all the wrong reasons. You could almost make an old black-and-white movie, a surreal horror type, out of it. But to this day I've never seen any of it on television, except a tiny clip on *A Question of Sport* – one of those 'What Happened Next?' things – they showed McNeill going up, apparently going to handle the ball. And of course what happened next is that Feyenoord scored the winning goal.

TOMMY GEMMELL After the Lisbon final we all got pissed; after the Milan final we all got pissed. For totally different reasons. There's nobody needs to tell us how disappointed the supporters were; but I assure you there was no one more disappointed than the squad of players.

GEORGE SHERIDAN The fans were okay. They kind of accepted defeat. There weren't any recriminations. I think they were just glad to get back to Scotland, to be honest. I mean, the weather was terrible as well! Talk about 'into the bargain'!

JAMES DUNBAR I was a child. I can remember sitting in the house bawling my eyes out.

Rangers finally achieved their European nirvana in 1972 in the Nou Camp Stadium, Barcelona. As in 1967 the two Old Firm sides went almost all the way together. In the end Rangers had the stage to themselves; having longed for sole possession of the spotlight the post-match scenes in Barcelona made some players and supporters wish they could have been removed from the glare.

. . . the referee wasn't familiar with the 'away goals' rule . . .

SANDY STRANG Rangers had played Rennes of France in the first round. They were then drawn against Sporting Lisbon – first leg at Ibrox, second leg in Lisbon. Final score after 180 minutes, 5–5. Extra-time played. Final score after extra-time, 6–6. The referee ordered a penalty shoot-out. Rangers lost the penalty shoot-out and went dejectedly back to the dressing-room to be informed by a UEFA official that the referee's decision on the penalty shoot-out had been revoked. The referee wasn't familiar with the 'away goals' rule; often forgotten in the euphoria.

ALEX MacDONALD Sporting Lisbon; that was horrendous. All you could hear were the drums, you know. I don't know whether it was the green and white hoops of Sporting Lisbon that kept us going. We went in and we thought that we were out; and all of a sudden John Fairgrieve came along and said that we were through; and everybody started buzzing about.

WILLIE JOHNSTON We were all sitting in the dressing-room thinking we were out – even Willie Waddell thought we were out – and a newspaper man came into the dressing-room and said, 'What are yous worried about?' We all says, 'Get to f***, you effing –'. He says, 'Yous are through. Away goals.' Nobody in the club had thought of it because it was a new law that had come in that season. So Waddell went off to argue with the referee; that was one thing that Waddell was good at, he would argue that black was white to get his club through.

That season it felt on a Saturday like we were always thinking of the following Wednesday, of the European match; and when we got past Sporting Lisbon that night we knew that we could possibly do it. All through that season the bosses did their homework, and that added to it; you'd get in on a Monday, 'Where's the boss?' 'He's in France, he's in Italy, he's in so-and-so . . .'

For the sake of peace and harmony in the home, please excuse Colin from school after the afternoon interval . . .

COLIN GLASS I got off school early to see the quarter-finals of that campaign, against Torino; 72,000, and Alex MacDonald scored more or less with his stomach. I remember the note my mother sent to the Depute Rector in school, saying, 'For the sake of peace and harmony in the home, please excuse Colin from school after the afternoon interval.' And I did a deal with her that if we got through I wouldn't go to the semi-finals, because that was the night before our O-Grade Arithmetic. I watched that live on TV and Rangers were absolutely fantastic. I passed my Arithmetic too.

ALEX MacDONALD I did score against Torino at Ibrox; it was just a follow-in actually. But it wasn't with the stomach. Chest area, I would say.

SANDY STRANG After Torino, it was Bayern Munich. Parallel with the semi-final against Bayern Munich, Celtic had Inter Milan in a European Cup semi-final. They drew both games 0–0, and Dixie Deans missed his penalty. The Rangers fans rubbed it in with this song: 'Who put the screws on the Rotterdam cruise? Dixie, Dixie.' Harsh, but I suppose that was the price you had to pay.

DENIS CONNAGHAN That penalty . . . if you talk to Dixie he'll remember exactly what he did. I can still see it. It was the second one, I think; all of a sudden it disappeared into the darkness.

TOMMY HYNDMAN Dixie Deans' penalty – the moonrocket over Janefield Street. He ballooned it that high I think a Zeppelin caught it. But it was some night; in 1972 Scottish football was at its strongest; two European semi-finals in the city on the one evening.

He gave everybody fish suppers just to get rid of us . . .

ANDY ROBERTSON We went into Quintiliani's chip shop in Larkhall on the road home from Ibrox. Celtic were playing Inter Milan the same night and it came to penalties. It was on the telly in the chip shop. Quintiliani turned round to me and he said: 'Andy, you make sure that everybody behaves.' See when Dixie Deans hit it over the bar, the whole place erupted. He gave everybody fish suppers just to get rid of us.

WILLIE JOHNSTON When we went to France, Lisbon and Torino, Colin Stein and I would play up the front and we were just kind of, 'Keep your foot in, keep their back four occupied'. When we went to Munich in the semi-final it was, 'Keep your foot in, keep their back four occupied, kick Beckenbauer.'

STUART DANIELS In those days European travel was nearly unheard of. Most of all I just remember the incredible crowds at Ibrox; when we beat Bayern Munich in the semi-final at Ibrox, and Franz Beckenbauer just chucking it, just booting the ball out, he couldn't handle the pressure. I think it just got to him. With that crowd, the sheer volume of noise behind the goal, even the big name players bottled it. We were in the final!

SANDRA LEWSEY We couldn't afford to go. There were 25,000 Rangers supporters there that day and you would have given your right arm to have gone. The men went. My dad would have died if he thought that I was going to Spain, to a football match for goodness' sake – I mean it was bad enough me going to Govan.

JOHN SLOWEY   A couple of my friends went. I was just at that age where my parents wouldn't let me go myself and they definitely wouldn't let me go with some of the older boys because they knew what they were like. I think it was £25, or something ridiculous like that, to go there for three days – match ticket, and – you know, a fiver to spend for three days, have a right good time!

LESLIE WHITE   I was at Barcelona, along with about 600,000 others who claim to have been there. I was 20. We started to hitchhike. I worked on the railways at the time and we got the train to France because we could get a free pass there; then we tried to hitchhike. We hitchhiked maybe about ten miles; then we said, forget this; we ended up getting the train again. The train was full of Rangers fans, all steaming.

Five Rangers supporters steaming in the bridal suite of a Barcelona hotel . . .

CHARLIE LOGAN   When we got there the hotel was double-booked; it was a joke, everything was double-booked, the whole town. We ended up in the Bridal Suite, five of us. Five of us Rangers supporters steaming in the bridal suite on the tenth floor of a Barcelona hotel. The atmosphere in the town before the game was fine – there was very little trouble. The trouble wasn't caused by religion; the trouble was that San Miguel was about 5p a bottle.

ALEX MacDONALD   There was a bit of atmosphere. I can't remember if it was the day of the game or if it was before it, but we were definitely in Spain, and the supporters came over to us just to show their appreciation and the police actually went for the supporters with their big batons – I'm talking about the big long sticks. I think that they were probably frightened because the Rangers took that many supporters away. They do stick together and they have got a habit of singing the songs I like; I'm not sure whether you can expect a foreign police force to like them just that much.

ANDY ROBERTSON   Barcelona was the biggest disappointment of my life. I'd been to every other game that year – and I missed it. We'd just arrived at the hotel and there was a wee boy, right well made, and he just opened his jacket and he'd a shoulder-holster there. He turned round and he just said, 'Protestant bastards'; so I should have known what we were in for.

The next morning we got up for our breakfast. It was the day of the game and we wanted to get ham, eggs and that. They brought us this wee continental breakfast, just a wee bit of bread and a pot of jam. We tried to explain to the wee girl, but we couldn't speak Spanish, she couldn't speak English. So I got up on the table and I started up like a pig, you know, snort, snort, snort – for ham. And the chicken – cluck, cluck, cluck – for eggs. She burst out laughing and we were all killing ourselves, but the manager kicked the door open, 'You make a fool of my girl?', went away, walked out, and walked in with a dozen polis. Straight to the jail.

We thought we were getting out at half-past four when the police came round to the cell. In fact it was the biggest insult I've ever had in my life; the police came to the cell and handed me an egg. My mate just lost the head, flung the egg at the wall and said, 'We asked for that about ten hours ago.' So when Rangers were kicking off the European Cup Winners' Cup Final, May the 24th, 1972, half-seven at night, me and my mate were playing push-ha'penny in Barcelona jail.

JOHN GREIG   Going to the game that night on the coach, we started to see all our supporters, with the colours and the flags and the scarves; all we could see was Rangers supporters. And by the time we arrived at the ground – and I'm not sentimental in any way – I had a lump in my throat. I thought, 'We really have to win it for them.'

COLIN GLASS   I was absolutely disgusted by the SFA banning the live coverage. Scotland were playing Wales that night. But there would have been fewer fans at Hampden Park than there were travelling to Barcelona. I listened to it in the back garden on my radio, then watched it at night, terribly, terribly excited.

GEORGE MacLEOD I tried to stay away from the radio; even though it was that important I wanted to see it as if it was 'as it happened'. Anyway, about an hour in I couldn't not tune in and I caught David Francey saying that Rangers were 3–0 up; I turned it off again so I would get the best of both worlds. But when I did watch it later on it was awful – I was smiling up to 3–0, then it went 3–1, 3–2 and I had no idea how it had finished.

SANDRA LEWSEY I remember the game very well – three up, then they came back to 3–2 and nerves were jangling.

JOHN GREIG I look back at that game – only a few years ago did I get a video of it – and I see what a terrible match it was. I always remember the last quarter of an hour; every time the referee blew his whistle I was hoping it was over because I was absolutely shattered. Then the fans started coming on the park and I kept looking at the referee. I'd been getting on quite well with him for most of the game and I kept saying, 'Fini, fini?' and he kept going.

WILLIE JOHNSTON We were praying for the final whistle because we were out on our feet – we were knackered. I remember running for the tunnel – there were steps coming up from the dressing-room and I'd just got down the steps and Colin Stein's standing there waiting on me. And he says, 'I thought you were supposed to be quick!'

COLIN GLASS The highlights were black and white. The whistle went round about 90 minutes and all the fans went on to the park. Then of course it wasn't the final whistle – so they'd to clear them off, play another minute and then the fans went on again. After that I can't recall seeing anything.

JOHN GREIG What I still can't understand was the Spanish police. It wasn't as if the Rangers supporters were coming on to take on some Russian supporters. It was basically Rangers supporters coming on to celebrate. They came on because they thought that the game was finished. The Spanish police clearly over-reacted.

STUART DANIELS I was on the pitch, so was my older brother. We're actually on the old black-and-white film. I'm about ten yards away from my older brother, and yet I never met him till after the game. The game ended, everybody rushed on, the police charged. I was the first to reach Alex MacDonald. He's been on the television, Alex, saying that I actually rescued him. I managed to lift him out and get him over the head; there were people pulling at his jersey, people mauling him, people saying, 'Give us his boots.'

We've done it, wee man, we've done it . . .

ALEX MacDONALD The crowd had a hold of me and I was struggling for air and this big fellow – big Stuart Daniels, a really good Rangers supporter – he was shouting, 'We've done it wee man, we've done it'; grabbing me, and – he's got three days of growth – scratching me, and I'm shouting, 'Stuart, I'm struggling here.' So he and a couple of his mates got me up and he filtered me over. I was really under pressure; that's the truth and that's what I remember – it's not the best of memories, is it?

JOHN GREIG The actual night was probably the biggest anti-climax in my life because it was as if we got through the back door to get something rather than going up the front steps.

WILLIE JOHNSTON To go up and lift the Cup in the Nou Camp, in that beautiful stadium, would have been special. But to get it presented in the dressing-room – 25 feet underground, it was like being in a bunker – well, that was it; everybody just had a wee look and put it in the corner.

SANDY STRANG It was a tainted euphoria. John Greig says to this day that it is one of his great disappointments that the trophy was presented inside the dressing-room. Instead of holding it aloft as Caesar had done in Lisbon, Greig had to be content with an official handing it to him in a dressing-room while the troops went about their riotous business outside.

CHARLIE LOGAN We stayed the night and we left the next morning. We'd heard all sorts of rumours that the Cup was being withheld, all that sort of stuff, so we were worried. The next morning we saw a picture of John Greig collecting the Cup underneath the stadium; we were just happy to know that we had it. But it was a bit of an anti-climax not seeing the team running round with the Cup. It was a bit of a shame.

ANDY ROBERTSON See when we were released from the jail? All the Spanish were applauding, shaking our hands and everything, 'Viva the Rangers, Viva the Rangers.' We walked up towards the stadium and all the Spanish fans were shaking our hands. We thought they were shaking hands because Rangers were winning, but they were shaking hands because the Rangers fans were laying in to the police, and they were terrified of the police because of the Franco regime.

LESLIE WHITE After the game we went back to the town, met a guy there, spent the night in his hotel room with maybe a dozen bottles of champagne and had a sing-song for the rest of the night. It was fantastic. But there were a lot of problems in Barcelona the next day. In the section they call the Ramblas, in downtown Barcelona, the police were just grabbing guys and pulling them into the car. So it was a case of, scarves off, sombreros on. We didn't get back till Saturday morning and we were still singing when we got back to Glasgow. We went straight to Hampden for the Scotland–England.

COLIN GLASS It was one of the big regrets of my life that I wasn't there. I did take the next day off school to see Rangers bringing back the European Cup Winners' Cup. It was pouring with rain.

BRIAN CRAIG When they came back and they got a lorry and went round Ibrox, we were there then. And you felt that that was just the end of the game, that that was the night they won it, when they came back to Ibrox and took the trophy round the stadium.

Above all, the 1965–75 period will be remembered as a time when Jock Stein ruled the Scottish football roost. Needless to say, the Celtic board marked his passing with an appropriately grand gesture. A seat on the board? A permanent memorial? No – an offer to join the PR team.

STEVEN GALL I think it goes without saying that to most Celtic fans Jock Stein is a bit of a god, a messiah – which I think is a bit heavy. But he did revolutionise Celtic with his ways and his tactics and produced teams that Celtic fans have never seen the likes of since.

GEORGE SHERIDAN It was like heaven, I suppose. With Jock Stein there you felt that you could do anything. Everyone just had this tremendous faith in Jock Stein, that he was never going to make any mistakes. There's a fellow I know – he summed it up quite well. He said that we were spoiled by the Stein Era – and everything else just pales into insignificance.

ADAM SHIELS I always thought that what they did to big Jock Stein was a disgrace; after all he'd done for the club, to be offered a PR job must have been a tremendous slap in the face. One of my photos shows it; big McNeill is taking over, and big Jock is there, and Billy and Desmond White are standing there as if shaking hands, and Jock's standing there, shoved to the back – all of a sudden he was thrown out the road.

TOMMY HYNDMAN It's a disgrace the way he was treated at the end but the supporters let him know what they thought of him before he went to Leeds. The Celtic fans let him know that he didn't build a team – he built the club. Jock Stein was like a god to most Celtic fans of my era. Kids growing up now hear this name, they see black-and-white footage, hear interviews. Bill Shankly was the only English manager that turned up at the European Cup final when Celtic won it in 1967 – and the great quote from Shankly when he went into the dressing-room afterwards was: 'John – you're immortal now.'

Chapter Seven

SONGS

The '60s and '70s were the great years for crowd-participation. Not only did singing arrive, to make the buzz of a crowd an even more excitingly communal experience than it had been before; not only were there terraces sufficiently populated with people full of the right spirit (and sometimes full of the right spirits) to sing lustily; not only was there a steady supply of new pop-tunes to adapt and mimic; but, above all, Glasgow football fans actually had something to sing about. Memories of thronged, singing terraces is one of the reasons why football of that period is looked back on with such nostalgia by the thirty-something generation.

The '60s followed a period of not much singing at all; not of a communal sort, anyway. Supporters sang on buses and at functions and in other impromptu ways ('One singer, one song, no refusals'). After the '60s, singing went on, though less inventively and creatively; in Glasgow the singing started to reflect the Irish troubles. In the '80s singing took on a more aggressive quality; now, in the '90s, the restrictions of the Taylor Report are threatening to put an end to singing altogether.

DOMINIC MURRAY Back in the '50s people didn't sing as much as they do now – it was more roaring. All right, the Rangers fans always sang 'The Sash' and 'Derry's Walls'; and at that time Celtic inclined to 'Follow, Follow' – 'Follow, follow, we will follow Celtic', which is a Rangers song now. In those days it was more roaring; the blokes would be shouting, 'Get intae him . . .' Just individuals shouting. There were songs going about but they were kind of ballads; they weren't tunes that you could chant. You'd hear them at a Celtic supporters dance, maybe:

> Said Lizzie to Philip as they sat down to dine
> I've had a letter from an old friend of mine
> His name is big Geordie, he's loyal and true
> And his lovely big nose is a rare shade of blue . . .

The 'Geordie' is George Young. In the song he's writing a letter to her for her to send up a cup for the Rangers to win, and he asks her to send Arsenal up to beat Celtic, to get them out of the way. Philip says something like:

> . . . there's only one thing
> You'd better watch out or the Celts might step in . . .

It goes on and on.

DOUGIE DICK Those kind of songs are still around. There's one I like that not many people know.

> There's a game called football, played in every land
> There's a team called Glasgow Rangers, they're fine and they are grand
> They've played in yonder meadow, in Europe, the USA
> But their greatest ever games have been played on New Year's Day.

But that's the sort of song you'll hear on a bus, not at a ground.

DENIS CONNAGHAN At Parkhead in the '50s it was all 'Hail Glorious St Patrick' and all that stuff; hymns and everything. What changed it all was that in Jock Stein's day Glen Daly – he was a great singer here, an Irish-Scottish guy – he brought in 'It's a Grand Old Team'; and Jock started to have it played before every match. The style switched from the old hymns to the modern stuff.

IAIN PATTERSON Once you get into the '60s you get much more organised singing, much more communal stuff. Friends

have told me that on the Ibrox terraces in the '60s the reper-
toire of songs was much greater than it is today. This included
Orange songs – for instance, 'The Green Grassy Slopes of the
Boyne', 'The Orange and the Blue' – songs you just don't hear
at Ibrox anymore. 'The Old Orange Flute' is another one. I
think there also seemed to be more spontaneous chants then.
They tended to take ideas from pop songs. I read in *Follow
Follow* of an event that happened in the late '60s. Rangers were
playing Hearts and during the match a guy called Rene Moller
of Hearts was putting himself about. At the end of the game
which I think finished 1–1 the Rangers fans broke into a spontaneous chant of:

> Don't walk away Rene
> You're gonna get f***ed on Wednesday.

DAVID POTTER They started singing Beatles things like
'Hey Jude' – 'Na, na, na, na-na-na-na, na-na-na-na, Cel-tic.'
And, from the Scaffold song:

> Thank you very much for the Glasgow Celtic,
> Thank you very much, thank you very, very, very much,
> Thank you very much for Jimmy Johnstone,
> Thank you very, very, very much.

And there was a lovely one in the early '70s:

> Aye, aye, aye, aye, we are the Glasgow Celtic
> Wherever we go we'll fear no foe,
> For we are the Glasgow Celtic.

Wait till I get this now:

> Aye, aye, aye, aye, Simpson is better than Yashin,
> And Wallace is better than Eusebio
> And Johnstone is better than anyone.

It was lovely, that.

STEPHEN MURRAY 'You'll never walk alone' they brought back from Liverpool. It's usually kept for times when the team needs a real lift, or in times of celebration in the days when we won a load of trophies. It would go into injury-time and the scarves would go up and you'd get the 'Walk On' which would culminate with the final whistle and the roar going up – it was tremendous.

When I was wee Harry Hood had just signed for Celtic; and Colin Stein signed for Rangers about the same time. I don't know how much Harry Hood cost – maybe about £30,000; but Colin Stein cost £100,000 from Hibs – a record, really big-time. At the next Celtic–Rangers game Harry Hood did really well and Stein didn't play awfully well. The Rangers fans were giving Colin Stein big licks; and finally the Celtic fans started singing:

> Harry Harry Harry Hood
> He's half the price but he's twice as good . . .

Things like that are priceless. Harry Hood had the right sort of name; not only Hood, which rhymes with everything; but also at that time there was the Hari Krishna thing – 'Harry, Harry, Harry, Harry, way-ay-oh, Harry, Harry.' Harry Hood had about five chants all to himself. He had the 'Jesus Christ Superstar' one:

> Harry Hood, superstar,
> How many goals have you scored so far?

Dixie Deans got that one of course after he missed the penalty against Inter Milan:

> Dixie Deans, superstar,
> Why did you put the ball over the bar?

But the main Dixie Deans one was just the 'Oh, Dixie, Dixie – Dixie, Dixie, Dixie, Dixie, Dixie Deans.' You could get right into that, with the big woah. – 'WOAH, Dixie, Dixie . . .'

The past – standing on the terraces and a wee bevvy . . .
(COLORSPORT)

'In those days, you had the wingers . . .'
Johnstone and Henderson, the last great number 7s
(COLORSPORT)

*'We're on our way to Lisbon': Celtic fans, including Adam Shiels (second row, centre),
set off from Hamilton for Lisbon, 1967*
(CHARLES McBAIN/ *THE HAMILTON ADVERTISER*)

John Greig is mobbed by invading fans at full-time in Barcelona, 1972
(COLORSPORT)

See no evil . . .
(COLORSPORT)

. . . the infamous Cup final of 1980
(COLORSPORT)

Changing times, but the same old allegiances
(COLORSPORT)

The fans speak. Celtic fans show red cards to Rangers' Scott Nisbet, 1988 . . .
(COLORSPORT)

. . . while Leeds receive a similarly encouraging message, 1992
(COLORSPORT)

The future – bucket seats and bluenose burgers
(COLORSPORT)

DOMINIC MURRAY Davie Provan was the first one I remember having the Guantanamera one – 'There's only one Davie Provan.' Tommy Gemmell had a lot of songs to himself, too – 'Gemmell's a bastard!' They were mainly sung by the Rangers fans. He used to say that he'd wake up in – was it Kirkintilloch where he lived? – and he'd hear the milk-boy singing 'Gemmell's a bastard!' at six o'clock in the morning!

JOHN BUTTERFIELD There was a chant you used to hear in the '60s, a version of that. Gemmell had scored an own goal against Russia – he hit it over Ronnie Simpson's head – and the chant was changed to 'Gemmell's a Russian!'

IAIN PATTERSON In the 1970s there were some songs that were taken – Abba's 'Super Trouper' became 'Super Cooper, Super Davie Cooper'; Queen's 'We Are The Champions' was sung with great gusto; Rod Stewart's 'Sailing' was taken by both sets of fans. I've been told that they even adapted Deep Purple's 'Black Night' to a Rangers song – I don't think you'll hear any Pink Floyd or Led Zeppelin now.

The big change in the '70s and '80s is that you started to get the more aggressive chanting. I wonder if the '70s was the only time when you got pro-violence songs and chants? That Gary Glitter thing, 'Hello, Hello' had various versions, like 'Hello, hello, any aggro, hello . . .' or 'A-G, A-G-R, A-G-R-O, Ag(g)ro!' And then there was 'Oh there won't be many going home' to the tune of 'She'll be coming round the mountain.' And of course at that time you get the standard response to a goal by the other side – 'You're gonna get your f***ing heads kicked in . . .'. There was some anti-police chanting, as well – 'If you hate the Glasgow polis clap your hands . . .' Both sides sang that.

The Ulster/Eire division of loyalties had, of course, always been represented in Celtic and Rangers terrace discographies, but with the troubles in Northern Ireland came a rise in chants and songs of contemporary relevance.

DAVID POTTER In 1963 I started to take an unhealthy interest in rebel songs. There was a man who sold a pirate magazine – the first ever fanzine? – called 'The Shamrock'. He was shabbily dressed, thin, emaciated and his shoes were down at the heel. I called him 'downtrodden man' from the rebel song 'Kelly the Boy from Killane'. In 1969 or thereabouts, when the Irish troubles started, the political stuff returned; things like 'One Man, One Vote' and various obscene things about Ian Paisley.

IAIN PATTERSON Friends have told me that in the early days of the troubles there were a lot of anti-Bernadette Devlin chants – she had recently been elected MP for mid-Ulster and had a high profile. In those days riots were more prevalent than shootings and the names of the Falls and the Shankhill were high profile areas in the news; and there was one song, 'I Was Born Under a Union Jack' which was sung to the tune of 'I Was Born Under a Wandering Star' by Lee Marvin:

> I was born under a Union Jack,
> I was born under a Union Jack.
> Do you know where hell is? Hell is in the Falls,
> Heaven's in the Shankhill and we'll guard old Derry's Walls,
> I was born under the Union Jack . . .'

MARGARET DEVLIN As far as Celtic goes they've always sung songs with an Irish slant, particularly the Irish national anthem. You did get people bringing in other songs, more political things. Their own fans drowned them out either by booing them or whistling or better still starting up a Celtic song, one which had real meaning for the club. I think it was more to the fore whenever Celtic played Rangers. You would get the two sides – Celtic singing their songs, Rangers singing theirs. Rangers don't really have any songs that aren't sectarian – 'We're up to our knees in Fenian blood' and all that.

IAIN PATTERSON Celtic fans would sing:

> *IRA all the way,*
> *F*** the Queen and the UDA.*

and Rangers fans would sing:

UDA all the way,
F*** the Pope and the IRA.

So that pretty much set their loyalties!

But in my experience the only time the troubles directly impinged on terrace chants was about the time of the hunger strikes. I remember one Old Firm game shortly after Sands was elected and shortly before he died when the Celtic End was full of stuff like 'Bobby Sands MP'. When he died was shortly before the Scottish Cup final against Dundee United and that match was punctuated by songs such as 'Bobby Sands, you're the Slimmer of the Year' and 'Could you go a chicken supper, Bobby Sands?' The night of the replay of that game I left Stirling at about five o'clock and got to Glasgow at about six. By the time we got to the match people were singing 'Two in a row, two in a row' – the second hunger striker had died on the afternoon of that day.

The outlook for a continued song-making creativity is uncertain, though new songs and chants appear practically every week.

DAVID POTTER   The crowds were very much more inventive as song-makers than they are now. There's too much obscene singing nowadays, you know – frankly quite offensive stuff – stuff that's really not funny – stuff like 'Ooh, aah, up your –' What's the point of that? There's not as much humour as there used to be. The patter of the supporters was always great – I always loved listening to that. If a high cross came across and John Hughes missed it – 'Aye, he would have needed a ladder to get that one.'

HUGH TONER   'I've seen a pint of milk turn quicker' – all that stuff. 'Right through the two backs! . . . Aye – and right into the midden.'

MICK MAHER   On an icy day at pre-electric blanket Tannadice, I remember big Roddy McDonald struggling along, and somebody shouted 'Haw, McDonald – the *Titanic* performed better on ice than you!' And there was a heated discussion going on about Dom Sullivan, and when someone suggested a lot of work was done off the ball, the reply came 'I've seen mair aff the ball running in Subbuteo.'

SANDY STRANG Often the humour has tended to be acerbic and harsh rather than amusing, but one time when McCoist came on as substitute during the Souness era (when McCoist was nicknamed 'The Judge' because he sat so often on the bench) Rangers were losing heavily and McCoist was chasing shadows. It was quite clear that he was pretty narked and he ran about and he was getting involved in little incidents that were totally out of character – and the Celtic fans from the Jungle started singing, 'Ally canny take it, Ally canny take it.' It was lovely.

COLIN LAMOND You probably find there's a better atmosphere among the Rangers crowd away from home because there are slightly fewer restrictions involved. There's more singing of the party songs. The party songs are constants – you get 'No Surrender', 'The Billy Boys', 'The Sash' – those'd be the main ones. You don't get them so much at home now that the whole ground's been seated, especially with the enclosure taken away – the East Enclosure was where the songs would generate from in the old days, but it takes a big event now for the whole stadium to get going. But the songs won't die. They'll lie dormant, and when they're needed to come back to be the twelfth man for the team, they will. When the team needs it, the crowd will be behind them.

WILLIAM JOHNSTON I remember 30-odd years ago when I was four or five and my dad first took me. The Derry, where the Rangers End was, was just immense. When you went into the Derry there was just a feeling you've never felt anywhere else; no matter what game you go to now you'll never get that feeling back. In those days you went in with your whole bus; your bus would be singing your songs and the next bus along would be singing their songs – and the place was just electric.

You were fighting against each other just to make sure you got your song in.

JOHN WATSON   It's because they split everybody up. It's no good anymore – you're not sitting with your mates anymore. I've got a season ticket; when I bought it ten years ago we went out and bought 20 tickets, me and my mates. We were all in a big group, we'd all travel together to Ibrox. But as things changed . . . now out of that 20 there's maybe only eight in that section – and some aren't my mates but guys they knew who bought them off them. So I'm there basically on my own; and you're not going to sit and sing in the way we would if there's a crowd of us together. That'll never come back.

STEPHEN MURRAY   What you might find happening is what happens in Italy, where there's always an end behind the goal where the fanatics go. Maybe the Jungle will remove itself to behind the goal. Or the club might designate a section, saying, 'If you want to go and sing then go to such and such a place.' In Italy it's only that little space that sings; the rest of the ground is all sitting still.

JOHN WATSON   You always get new songs – I don't know who makes them up – but like if something goes wrong a new song will always rise up. When McStay missed the penalty against Raith Rovers, the next week it was:

> . . . Paul McStay
> Missed a penalty . . .

Somebody'll always start something – 'Could you go a Coca-cola, Paul McStay?'

JOHN BUTTERFIELD   I made it to the first Old Firm game of 1994–95 – a glorious occasion it was too. One amusing chant was directed at Duncan Ferguson:

> He's tall, He's skinny,
> He's going to Barlinnie,
> Ferguson, Ferguson . . .

SANDY STRANG   I heard some Rangers supporters coming out of a bar singing, 'Hello, hello, we are the Boli boys' which recognition of Basile Boli I quite liked. I also heard someone referring to him as Billy Boli!

JOHN WATSON   You always want opposition fans there; for any big games you want a few of them there, because you want them to go away remembering you. You're playing your part and you want them to go away saying, 'Did you hear those fans? They never shut up . . .' When you read in the paper that the Rangers fans never stopped singing for 90 minutes you go away thinking, 'F***ing brilliant'.

Players, though not always aware of what is happening off the pitch, do appreciate the chanted support directed at them.

WILLIE JOHNSTON   I loved to hear a crowd – especially when we were winning. I enjoyed the 'Willie, Willie, Willie, Willie Johnston on the wing' and all this. When you were playing away and they were shouting 'Johnston, you're a junkie, Johnston you're a bastard, Johnston you're a so-and-so' – that was when you knew you were getting on top of them, that you could still do the business.

MURDO MacLEOD   I had a great thing with the supporters. There's a wee story that was put in a magazine when I left Celtic and went to Dortmund. Whenever they got a free kick they used to chant my name . . . 'Murdo, Murdo, Murdo, Murdo' – the Big Ben thing. When I was with Dortmund and I came back and played Celtic, and there was a free kick to Celtic, they started to chant my name – which I thought was a nice one. They beat us 2–1 on the night, and the Jungle started to sing 'Murdo, Murdo.' It started to spread round and it was a wee bit emotional; I had to get off the park because the tears were coming down and so on.

   The next time Dortmund played Celtic at Celtic Park I was doing the television; I was playing with Hibs by that time. I was doing it from the gantry up the top, and when I was walking round the Dortmund fans were all singing my name; and as I walked by the Jungle the Celtic fans were all singing my name. These are the wee things that make it all worthwhile; that tell you you belong.

Chapter Eight

TROUBLE and STRIFE
1975–1985

1975–76 was a season of change in Scottish football. The old-style First and Second Divisions were disbanded. In their place came a structure topped – if that is the right word – by the Premier League, grandly, and perhaps laughably, modelled on the German Bundesliga example. So we were told at the time, anyway. The idea was to create a superbreed of Scottish players who were constantly involved in meaning-ful games; what it seems to have achieved is such a plethora of meaningful games that players focus all their efforts on depriving each other of the time and space to play. The ulti-mate failure of this initiative has been most fully witnessed recently, with suggestions for new structures arising yearly (depending, usually, on the self-interest of the proposer) and with the system carrying some of the can with regard to Scottish failures in Europe.

At the time, though, it relieved the Old Firm and the other big sides of fixtures which did not always challenge them. Jock Stein's celebrated half-time team talk, which offered a bonus for turning a 3–0 lead into something much larger on a pounds per goal basis, was put back in the bottom drawer. It did seem to engender a world in which, at the turn of the '80s, Aberdeen and, to a lesser extent, Dundee United, could take power. At the same time it encouraged middling teams to play ultra-defensive football. Hibs, for instance, who under Eddie Turnbull had been an attractive side who could rattle up a few goals while keenly chasing Stein's Celtic, were transformed into a side of 0–0 battlers, their bodies strung haplessly across the midfield.

. . . everybody getting on the cattle-train, as they called it . . .

JOHN SLOWEY   We – Rangers – won the last old First Division, when we ended the nine-in-a-row, and the first Premier League. Before it changed you were visiting places like Arbroath, East Fife, Dunfermline. It was always a really good day out – set off early in the morning, everybody getting on the cattle-train, as they called it, having a wee drink, getting to the destination quite early, try to sneak in for a beer. When the Premier League came in it became a bit boring.

MARGARET DEVLIN   A lot of the games were meaningless in the old league, a waste of time – you were just thumping these teams, the Clydes and Arbroaths and Stirling Albions. But when it came on to the new Premier League, the so-called Elite League, and you had to meet the same teams four times in the season and it got to the stage where teams knew you, you knew how they played – it became dull. So many teams came to Celtic Park to defend.

HARVEY BEATON   You maybe had twenty teams and you were maybe playing Queen of the South – it was a crap game but you had a social, a bevvy, you'd be talking to the guy next to you. You'd say, 'Who was that scored there, the fourth one, who scored?'

COLIN GLASS   The introduction of the Premier League – the end of the fixtures against the Queen of the Souths and the Arbroaths – was definitely an improvement. I remember going to one game at Ibrox between Rangers and Arbroath. Colin Jackson, who rarely ever scored, scored from about 30 yards and Rangers won 3–0. There were only about 16,000 there, the atmosphere was terrible, and I thought who, except for the diehards, is ever going to come and watch this?

FRANK MOOTY   I found it sad when it changed. I thoroughly enjoyed the games against the smaller teams; the likes of Third Lanark, Arbroath, Queen of the South. I liked the football magic kind of thing.

GORDON SMITH   It was a period of magic hairstyles, that's for sure. John Greig had the little goatee beard, but that was a bit before my time. I think big Derek Johnstone's was the worst, the curly perm; I remember him sporting that prior to the '78 World Cup.

The first five years of the '70s brought mixed fortunes. Under Jock Wallace, Rangers won two Trebles; they were denied a third when, with John Greig in charge, they lost the League to a Celtic side who had to rebuild under Greig's old adversary, Billy McNeill.

. . . born is the King of Ibrox Park . . .

IAIN PATTERSON One of the principal figures of the Wallace teams was Derek Johnstone. Derek started at centre-forward and that's where he should have stayed, but he moved to centre-half. I can't remember the game but in the late '70s there were fights at Ibrox between Rangers supporters. I remember one game when maybe half the crowd – was singing 'There's Only One Derek Johnstone,' while the other third was singing 'Parlane, Parlane, Parlane, Parlane – born is the King of Ibrox Park,' because they were sort of contesting for the number nine shirt. I think Parlane might have been the better footballer but Johnstone scored the goals.

GORDON SMITH The two Dereks – Johnstone and Parlane – got on great. Parlane was a good guy. He accepted he wasn't a regular in the team, and he would often come in and score a vital goal as a substitute.

The Treble team was extraordinary; a privilege to have played in it. Things happened that you'd just dream about, because people could play. You made a run and the ball got delivered, that was the great thing, with Cooper and McLean out wide. We'd a back four and all four of them had captained Scotland – Jardine, Jackson, Forsyth and Greig.

The Wallace period was a period of transition at Celtic Park. The Quality Street Kids, a group of young players who had learned the game in the shadow of the Lisbon Lions, were allowed to depart.

JOHN LARKIN   That was a period that Celtic had such a boring team; there were players there that should never have been there when they had people like Edvaldsson. I seemed to lose interest.

. . . he used to drink Barr's Irn Bru after training . . .

JOHN BUTTERFIELD   I lost interest a bit when I was about 14. Celtic's fortunes slipped. They had made some bad signings, and I lost enthusiasm for the game. I came back later on – late '70s, when they had George McCluskey; I remember reading an article where it said that he used to drink Barr's Irn Bru after training; and when he gave it up he said he lost a stone. But he's still playing, so maybe there's something in Barr's Irn Bru. The elixir of youth.

GEORGE MOORE   Stein left us what wasn't a very good team, and there were a lot of bad times after that; John Dowie, Graham Sinclair, Joe Filippi.

TOMMY GEMMELL   There was a player called Joe Filippi; big Jock brought him up from Ayr towards the end of his time there; not the greatest signing. He was on the bench one day at Celtic Park and Jock told him to warm up; so away Joe went, doing his stretches and a few sprints, limbering up and all that sort of stuff. So Jock calls him back and when he got back to the dug-out and Jock's giving him his instructions he says, 'By the way, why did you go and loosen up at the Rangers End?' 'Because I get less f***ing stick there,' he said.

DANNY McGRAIN   I signed up with Dalglish, Macari, Davidson, Cattanach. We were known as the 'Quality Street Kids', and we trained with the Lisbon Lions, a great learning experience. They were not all angels; one or two were bevvy merchants. But they'd all come in after having a session and they'd train till they dropped. Myself and Kenny used to be at the back when we ran round the track as a warm-up in twos – 30-odd players, a big squad. And some days the waft of vodka and Bacardi and whisky would rise up – you thought, a good night last night again. It was sad when the Quality Street Kids drifted away. It meant that Celtic had a poor time of it until 1979 – the 4–2 game.

MURDO MacLEOD It was big Billy's first season. Some time in the winter everything seemed to gel; the team wanted to fight for one another and everyone within the dressing-room knew we could win the League that year even though we were so many points behind. It was a bad winter and we ended up having about six games in hand. We had to play St Mirren; and then we had to play Rangers, basically for the Championship. They'd won the League Cup and were in the Scottish Cup final; so this was the Treble for them.

. . . they're all going daft again and I'm going, 'Somebody up there hates us . . .'

STEPHEN MURRAY I was in first year. You talk about a build-up – there was some build-up that day. Celtic had come from nowhere, they're all talking about it, the whole school's buzzing with it; my dad said it was the same in the shipyards. My dad went off for a pint and said that the bus was leaving from outside the pub at half past six, to make sure I was there because it wouldn't wait for me; I was there at half-past five, paranoid that they'd miss me when they came out the pub. So we're on the bus; the atmosphere really gets going on the bus; some guys are trying to sing and others are talking about the game and that. There's a point you come to on the bus when you're as well jumping off and walking because the bus can't get any further; it's crawling along. You get out and walk up and you're really in the thickness of the crowd, all walking up to the ground. It was a beautiful night; a warm, evening, about 60 or 70 degrees in the day and it held it in the evening, no breeze. Beautiful – till Rangers scored.

I was wee and standing at the front and you know what it's like; the crowd's all singing and your ears are bursting. Alex MacDonald scored; I heard that ball hit the net; a shhhhh-noise. A horrible feeling. The funny thing was that there was a delayed reaction at the Rangers End, a couple of seconds and then – YEAH! – the whole place went mental. One-nil at half-time; we'd hit the bar twice and Johnny Doyle sent off.

When they say the crowd gets behind the team; it happened

that night. Aitken equalised and you got hope; you saw a wee light at the end of the tunnel. And then McCluskey whacks one in off Jackson – 2–1 for Celtic. It just erupted; and do you know, the Celtic fans were still in full voice when Rangers equalised. I'm going, 'Somebody up there hates us'.

DANNY McGRAIN   The ball came to Bobby Russell and I'm at the right-hand post; I thought it was going to go by so I let it go by; next thing I knew it was in the back of the net. I thought – 'They're going to get the Championship, and it's my fault . . .'

DOMINIC MURRAY   Two-each was enough for them; and they're all singing 'The only time that yous can sing is when you're in the chapel . . .' They belted it right out. That was the worst thing they could have done. Cause, here, it started – 'Celtic, Celtic, Celtic!' It drowned them out – and The Celtic Song started. And the third goal came. That was it. And then, injury-time, MacLeod gets the ball, and everyone where we were standing are all shouting, 'Hit it anywhere!' – even McNeill in the dug-out was shouting, 'Hit it anywhere!' – and he hit it right into the top corner. The crowd went mad, it erupted. We were all singing 'Ten Men Won the League' and all that – to the tune of 'Brown Girl in the Ring'.

MURDO MacLEOD   I picked it up sort of mid-way; but I thought if I'm not going to score I'll make sure the ball-boys have got to go and run and get it! It went over Peter McCloy into the top right-hand corner.

SEAMUS MURPHY   I was working at Vauxhall's in Luton and couldn't get time off. I was working night shift – 8 p.m. to 7 a.m. – working on the line spot-welding car-bodies. My mate Bill Muldoon, who was in Quality Control at the end of the line, about 50, 60 feet away, gave me through sign language that Rangers were one up, then that Celtic were down to ten men, then the equaliser, then Celtic ahead, then the equaliser. Then nothing . . . my head was in a spin. I had four weld guns on each car and you had about one and a half minutes on each car; how I managed to keep the welds perfect I'll never know. I kept look-ing up to Bill – no signs. My stomach was churning and to top it all our foreman, Big Bill MacPherson, was a hun and was watching me. After an eternity Bill stuck his hands up and gestured 4–2. I assumed Rangers had won . . . then a big grin spread on his face from ear to ear. MacPherson was in a foul mood the rest of that night.

GORDON SMITH We blew it. I can't remember anything about the game. We sat shell-shocked in the dressing-room, thinking, 'What have we done?' knowing that Celtic were doing laps of honour and all the rest of it outside. A complete disaster.

We did go on and win the Cup; we played Hibs in a three-game series. Two 0–0 draws – awful, diabolical, dreadful games – and then we won 3–2 in the third game. I always remember the third game; 2–2 in extra-time and Davie Cooper got to the bye-line and chipped one over. I was right underneath it and I knew I was going to score. And Arthur Duncan, who was a Hibs' full-back by that time, bundled me out the way – then headed it smack into his own net. I remember shouting to him at the time – 'Let me score, ya bastard!' He's going to be lumbered for life with scoring the own goal winner in the Cup final; I could have scored it for him! I'll never forgive Arthur for that.

The 1980 Scottish Cup final was another of McNeill's successes, but it was not remembered as such. A day of disgraceful scenes on Hampden's hallowed turf led to a major change in the ethos and manner of Scottish fan behaviour.

IAIN PATTERSON The 1980 final was a reasonable game. Celtic won with a very lucky goal; McGrain hit a shot from about 35 yards and it flicked off McCluskey and sent McCloy the wrong way. It seemed, at least from the Rangers End, to crawl over the line; you felt like you could almost go on there and push the ball away.

DANNY McGRAIN It was a terrible, terrible game. I'm glad I was playing, not watching. I suppose I had a part in the goal in the sense that I was the second last person to hit the ball. I hit it – I mishit it, actually. I kicked it, anyway, and George McCluskey toed it. Poor Peter McCloy was already on his way to get the ball for a bye-kick, running, 'quick, get the ball up the park' kind of thing.

TOMMY HYNDMAN There was a late Danny McGrain strike that nobody could believe; it came off George McCluskey, sailed by the Govan Lighthouse – or something that sounds like that – big Peter McCloy – the onion bag bulged, and the place just erupted. And what I can remember – I don't know whether this is just through green-and-white tinted glasses or whatever – all the kids went down to try and get a grab at the players and the hooligan element at the other end just went bananas and surged forward. So the guys maybe about my age – 15, 16 and guys older than that – we weren't having that. So we all flew forward. I never actually got on to the park because my brother was pulling me back – 'Come here!' What you saw was like a gang fight you'd see then in Glasgow in the early '70s.

> *. . . people had the wide flared trousers, and they tended to put cans of beer and bottles of Pomagne underneath . . .*

IAIN PATTERSON In the '70s there were always signs saying 'No Alcohol' – but people took in masses of drink. I think ironically enough the fashions of the time helped them to do it; people had the wide flared trousers and they tended to put cans of beer and bottles of Pomagne underneath. So there was always a lot of alcohol swilling around the ground at that time.

The riot started when some Celtic fans invaded the park – mostly in celebration. At the start most people at the Rangers End weren't that fussed. I think it was after they encroached on Rangers territory – after they crossed the half-way line, or when they reached the 18-yard box at the Rangers End – that the trouble broke out. The police on horses came round from the Celtic End and tried to put the Celtic fans back into their area. At the Rangers End the battle wasn't between Rangers fans and Celtic fans, it was between Rangers fans and the police; I can remember just how black with bottles and cans it was when the police did come round. There's a very good description of this by David Francey on the radio commentary.

STEVEN GALL What you saw was tank tops and flares flying about; wedges going up in the air! The old scarves, tied around the wrists. People trying to punch and getting caught by the side, not getting the hook in. If it hadn't been so serious it would have been a funny sight, that final; two sets of fans clashing on the park, all real cool dudes, to coin a phrase, so long as they had two scarves around the wrists and the tank top and the big-lapelled shirt and the flares flapping in the wind. Hampden Park must have been a bit of a mess after all those platform shoes treading all over it!

JOE SHEVLIN   It was horrific at the finish – individual battles and the policewoman with the baton hitting people left, right and centre.

DANNY McGRAIN   The crowd were baying for us to go on to the park at time-up but the police told us not to go on. We went to the dressing-room. We had the champagne, the bath, whatever, and tales started coming in that there was a battle on the park; but you couldn't see in your mind's eye what they were talking about. We made our way to the bus and saw the ambulances and whatnot flying about. Later that night we saw it on TV; what can your reaction to be anything like that?

I don't think there's a picture of Celtic with the Scottish Cup that year . . .

MURDO MacLEOD   After the game we went back to the Grosvenor Hotel and there was a meal on – singing, drinking and celebrations – and it wasn't until we were in the hotel we were told that there was any crowd trouble. All we'd been told was that we weren't allowed a lap of honour. It'd be interesting to know if this is true, but I don't think that there's a picture of Celtic with the Scottish Cup that year.

GEORGE MacLEOD   The sequel to that game was of course the Criminal Justice Act, or whatever it was called; the new regulations; no drink to the ground, no drink on the buses, no drunks in the ground, all the rest of it. It changed everything.

JOE SHEVLIN   The time when the licensing laws were changed and they were not allowed to bring alcohol into football, they used to put these big bins outside. Of course the policemen stopping the fans bringing the alcohol in filled up these bins. So you'd have these bins full of confiscated drink.

Everyone was going home with their pockets full of half-bottles of whisky, wine, cans of beer.

JAMES DUNBAR   The difference in the drinking laws after the Hampden Riot made a difference. People were much more reserved. I can remember being at European nights when I was quite young, and my feet never touching the terracing; you were squeezed up in the crowd in the Jungle, for instance. That didn't happen any longer. You didn't get that sort of hysteria within the crowd.

MARGARET DEVLIN   People drank more in the stand than anywhere else, though it was more upmarket – they had their hip-flasks. The one thing I will say against the stopping of the drink is that – well, the women who went had their flasks too, but it was flasks of soup. On a very cold winter's day a flask of soup was nice – but it got to the stage where you couldn't take that in with you. As well as being a flask it was also an 'object'. Can you imagine me firing an object at somebody? No chance.

DANNY McGRAIN   It was one of the best things that happened because nobody was killed and all the non-drinking stuff came in. Though you'd like to have seen the changes without the riot.

   ... Oh let's in-vade the park, oh let's in-vade the park ...

IAIN PATTERSON   The year after the 1980 Cup final the police all came out. The previous year there had only been about eight police on the pitch when the riot happened; the next year they had policemen two feet apart, right round the semicircle. The Rangers fans started singing, 'Oh let's in-vade the park, oh let's in-vade the park ...'

Things had started to go wrong for Rangers after Jock Wallace stepped aside to let a younger man take the helm. When things turned sour on the younger man, John Greig, he stepped aside to let the older man back in for a second spell. A similar musical chairs routine was to follow at Celtic Park; they were as clear symptoms of bad times as spots on a measles-case.

TOMMY HYNDMAN   Rangers couldn't win the toss of the coin at that time; they'd built the new stadium the wrong way round, it was facing the pitch. I don't know if you remember the Drybrough Cup, it was one of these stupid wee summer tournaments that they used to stick out the reserve teams for. I remember, we were at Hampden and Rangers won 1–0, Davie Cooper scored; and Rangers did a lap of honour with the Drybrough Cup. That's how bad it was for them then.

JOHN SLOWEY   That time sticks with you – maybe because it was bad, maybe because I was at an impressionable age then, between, say, 16 and 24, when you're right into it. If you're not winning anything it sticks with you. That mob were gubbing us every time. They were pumping us! John Greig scored for us in the Glasgow Cup final and the bastards started clapping him! The whole Celtic End – I was guttered for the geezer – he's run 35 yards and burst the net and they start clapping.

. . . the dressing-room split into three or four factions . . .

DAVID McKINNON   When I went there the atmosphere in the dressing-room was one of the best; but when the results didn't come, the dressing-room split into about three or four factions. And then they started arguing. There was arguing behind the scenes; there was arguing on the pitch; and the fans started getting on our back. Certain players said to themselves, 'If I've not got the ball, I can't make mistakes and the crowd can't shout at me.' There were times I was getting the ball and I was looking up and there was nobody to find. So I would end up hitting an aimless ball towards their goal, and the fans were booing me, giving it 'a load of rubbish' and this and that.

IAIN PATTERSON   A lot of the crowd left – they voted with their feet. I think in many ways the decline was accepted, but obviously there were the after-match demonstrations against John Greig which took place just before he resigned; I have to admit to my shame I took part in one of these, though I don't think he should have been treated like that for what he did for the club. The more militant Rangers supporters took part. I remember outside – it wasn't just 'Greig Must Go' – there were various paramilitary songs, etc., so it wasn't your bowler hat types who were there.

I remember seeing the strain on his face . . .

SANDY CLARK   The demonstrations against John Greig I found sad; I found it disappointing that football supporters can be that way. It it made me appreciate how nasty football can be. To me John Greig was a true blue Ranger, a fabulous manager, a very, very good coach and very much underestimated. I remember seeing the strain on his face; you could see it maybe at half-time in certain games if you were losing. The crowd were restless too. At that time Rangers would sometimes have eight, nine, ten thousand people; I'm not sure of the exact numbers. There wasn't the same volume; but if they wanted to give criticism believe me you could hear them. They got to the manager.

STUART DANIELS   Rangers are now carrying about 15,000 fairweather fans. A lot of people used to say to me in pubs and clubs and what have you, back in the John Greig time, 'You're not going down there today, are you? You're aff your heid.' There's a hell of a lot of Rangers supporters sat in pubs and clubs and followed the snooker and the tennis, but they're all back there now. I dare say that's because people follow a winning side. Success has got a thousand fathers, you know.

MARK DINGWALL   Amongst my circle of supporters, we used to say that the Rangers were always better when your dad was a boy.

GEORGE MacLEOD   The return of Jock Wallace was hardly a forward step. He wasn't the man he was, I don't think; I know it's easy to say that now. I suppose at the time I was hopeful that he might be able to turn things around a little.

GORDON SMITH   Jock Wallace was a great man for appreciating football, contrary to his reputation. He used to come in and enthuse even about the training games – he'd come in and say, 'That was some game today, what about that pass . . .'

   He was kind of a frightening guy; kind of rough, kind of gruff. But again, contrary to what you'd think, he didn't give out a load of stick. Rather than saying something to you directly he'd get the message through to you via someone else. He might say to Tommy McLean, 'Tommy, I want you to play balls in behind the full-back because Smithy will run all day.' So I would hear that; and it was only years later that I realised that he was telling the other players your value.

There was a wee rhythm; on a Friday he'd get the wee men out on a board.

SANDY CLARK   Jock inspired a sort of fear. He was doing a tactics talk before the game down in the boot-room and he had the Subbuteo players out and he's saying, you play there, you play there. So he's got all these men out on the park and he's naming them, one, two, three – right up to 12. And everybody's sitting there, this full squad of professional players, the biggest names in Scottish football, too terrified to say that he had 12 players on the park. No way was anyone going to say, 'Who isn't playing?'

Wallace's return saw one outstandingly stylish win, soon after his return, when Rangers took the League Cup from Celtic in dramatic circumstances with a significant contribution from a slip of a lad named Alistair McCoist.

JIMMY NICHOLL   I enjoyed that Cup final, with the McCoist hat-trick. I think that was the time when I was only going to be there for six months; and I thought that I was going back to Canada. I thought, 'I'll never be back here, and I'm walking away here with a League Cup medal for Rangers having beat Celtic' – and after the atmosphere in the dressing-room when I'd arrived, that was something.

SANDY CLARK   In '84 we played a League Cup final; we played Celtic and won 3–2; Ally McCoist got the three of them. In the semi-final we played Dundee United and won over two legs. In the second leg I scored what was probably the best goal of my career, never mind for Rangers; I took it on my chest outside the area, turned and hit a volley across the goalkeeper. Very unusual for me. I've still got it on tape. The final was great for Alistair McCoist; it set him on his way to hero status. It wasn't so long since the fans had been on his back, giving him dog's abuse.

The atmosphere was fantastic, because we didn't ever win anything . . .

ALAN GALLOWAY   The first match I remember was the '83 or the '84 Skol Cup final – when we weren't doing particularly well. Ally McCoist scored a hat-trick; two penalties; and they beat Celtic 3–2. I was at the Rangers End at Hampden. I remember that game because it was unwatchable; the 90 minutes and the extra-time was spent trying to stand on your feet, with all the swaying. The atmosphere was fantastic, because we didn't ever win anything. Just winning, just thinking this was our day . . . whereas now nearly every day is our day, if you know what I mean.

The early '80s saw the arrival of 'The New Firm' – Aberdeen and Dundee United. Only a certain geographical proximity saw them stuck together under this label – in truth their achievements were markedly different, with Aberdeen winning a whole clutch of trophies and Dundee United far fewer. They did, however, give the Old Firm a hard time and they are not remembered as popular visitors.

JOHN SLOWEY   It didn't seem to matter how well Rangers played, Aberdeen always seemed to outdo us. Aberdeen gave us a few doings – I seem to remember a 5–1, some fours, some threes. The culmination was Aberdeen winning the Scottish Cup for the third time in a row. We were winning 1–0 and Alex McLeish of all people scored a goal from about 30 yards. These were dark days because you really expected to beat teams like Aberdeen – and here they were outfighting you, outplaying you and more than that embarrassing you with the scoreline. Two–one would have been bad enough. But four? Hard to stomach.

DAVID POTTER   The early '80s, with the rise of the New Firm, brought a feeling that things were more competitive. When you listened to the results you had to listen not just to the Rangers score but to the Aberdeen and Dundee United scores as well.

STEPHEN MURRAY   I remember the day Dundee United won the League. Celtic were playing Rangers at Ibrox, and it seemed really strange that someone else was going to win it.

JOHN SLOWEY   That New Firm period's actually left a legacy today. Now you very rarely get a really good atmosphere at Ibrox; the only game now you get atmosphere, present day, is Celtic. But also Aberdeen, and I think that's because there was that period when they kept turning us over. They played that red line charge from the penalty box and we were always getting caught offside. Gordon Strachan was the main instigator – I think everybody hated him in Scottish football at that time.

NEIL McDERMOTT   The New Firm? I'm not – what's the word I'm searching for? – altruistic enough to want to see other teams do well. People said, 'Oh, it's nice to see other teams winning.' Being totally pro-Celtic, the only thing I could say is that if we're not going to win it we prefer Aberdeen or Dundee United – anybody except Rangers!

Trips to Aberdeen and Dundee should perhaps have been more appreciated, because there was little in the way of more exotic distraction in this period. By the mid-'70s Glasgow's star as a European power had faded. In spite of the generally low level of success, however, there were memorable nights and experiences at home and away. The abstemiousness being legally enforced at matches in Scotland appears to have held little sway on trips south.

STEPHEN MURRAY   One year Celtic played Sachsenring of East Germany. We drew 1–1 at Parkhead. The return game was in the afternoon and it was live on the telly. My teacher had it up there, though; there were maybe 30 in the class there in the morning and she says, 'How many of you are intending to watch the Celtic game this afternoon?' Nobody had the courage to put up their hands. 'That's good,' she says, 'I'll expect you all in in the afternoon. No excuses about being off sick so you can watch it in the house.' And all the faces dropped. 'But I'll tell you what,' she says. 'If you all bring in ten pence then I'll open up the TV room on the top landing and the ten pences can go towards the missions.' And we're all, 'Oh, yes!' So I ran home to my ma and I said, 'Give me ten pence.' She said, 'What's it for?' I said, 'It's for the black babies.' She still doesn't know it was for watching Celtic.

GORDON INGLIS   European matches stick out in my mind as the biggest occasions. When Rangers were 1–0 down to

Juventus and had to score two at Ibrox, I was sitting in the old Centenary stand, which as a celebration of 100 years of the club was a bit ramshackle – benches and tin roofs slammed together with a few nails and screws. But the atmosphere that night was one I'll never forget.

GORDON SMITH I scored the winner that knocked Juventus out. Juventus had nine internationals, and practically the whole team had just come back from the 1978 World Cup. We got a £200 bonus for winning that match. An incredibly small amount. You didn't get rich playing for Rangers in those days. We beat PSV and got to the quarter-finals against Cologne; it came at a bad time. We lost 1–0 away and drew 1–1 at home; one of those sickening ones when the away goal goes in. We lost it early on, right enough, but we knew we'd not get three. A shame; I thought we could have won the European Cup that year.

IAIN PATTERSON In Cologne there was this rabbi standing about. This big bear goes over to him and says, 'Don't worry, mister, we'll get them that did it to you.'

HARVEY BEATON The Cologne fans were good; any time you meet them they want to swap you scarves. You never have any trouble at all in Germany. It always seems to be Portugal and the Catholic countries you have trouble in, because what seems to happen is it gets well documented in the press what Rangers represent, so by the time you get there they're growling.

STEPHEN MURRAY My dad took me to a European game one night; it was against Innsbruck, round about 1978. I was small. I said, 'Can my pal come?' He says, 'All right, go and tell your pal he can come.' So we got on the bus to the ground and there's a big queue coming back; there was always a good crowd for a European game, maybe 40, 50,000. Hundreds and hundreds of people around us. So it came to paying and my dad says, 'I canny lift the two of you over.' He looks around to see if he can see any of his pals; but he can't so he turns round to the guy behind and says, 'I've got two kids here, would you give one of them a lift over?' And the guy shows him his sleeve and says,

'I would, mate, but I've only got one erm.' The only one-armed guy in the whole stadium that night and he chooses him.

ADAM SHIELS   One of the worst displays of the supporters was at Burnley round about 1978 – we hadn't won anything so we had to go into the Anglo-Scottish Cup. It was enough to put you off football for the rest of your days. It started with the Burnley boys taunting the Celtic supporters. The Celtic bit was paling-ed off, and we were jam-packed in this corner, and the next thing these railings got pulled down and they were throwing them – they were actually using them as spears. They went berserk that night for some reason; by that time a lot more drink had come into the football.

JIMMY FINNIS   Rangers had to play in it one year, too; they lost to Chesterfield.

HARVEY BEATON   Chesterfield. You forget these things because they were so bad.

JAMES DUNBAR   Real Madrid was a tremendous game. Celtic totally dominated and Johnny Doyle scored. I was maybe 15 or 16, dogging off from school early because we came from Saltcoats and we'd to come up on the train. Myself and my mate actually went to Madrid. We got caught by the headmaster as we left St Andrew's Academy in Saltcoats; he was at the gate, asking us where we were going with the Celtic scarves. We said we were heading for Madrid, and it was a case of, 'I'll see you when you get back'.

We left from Ardrossan on the Garryowen bus; it had its first toilet stop in Dalry, which was only eight miles away – only about 2,000 miles to go! Stopping at service stations all the way through France to stock up on the booze . . . It was about 20 to a room in some Madrid hotel because only about two lads had booked accommodation; the rest of the lads all slept on the floor of the hotel. Up on the top tier of the stadium, it was tremendous. Coming back wasn't much cop; we'd lost 3–0.

JIMMY FINNIS   A friend told me this story. He was taking the sleeper down to London on the Monday before the Real Madrid game; and two minutes before the train leaves no one has arrived to to take the other bunk in the compartment, so he's thinking, great, a restful night. Then, just faintly, he hears the singing coming up the platform – 'Oh it's a grand old team to play for . . .' – and into the compartment come two guys. One ticket, of course; and no passports. Anyway, after they pull out a massive carry-out my friend decides that he's not going to get any sleep, that he might as well join them, and they drink all through the night. And about five in the morning one of them is sick into the sleeper compartment sink, all down the front of his Celtic replica shirt. So he takes the shirt off, throws it out the window and opens his suitcase. And all he's got in the suitcase is another pair of replica shirts – nothing else at all. The travelling supporter's kit.

Another one was Politechnica Timisoara; from the same city where the Romanian revolution started. What I remember was that their goalkeeper had the misfortune to be wearing an orange jersey; he couldn't work out why every time he kicked the ball he was getting booed; every time he went near it the booing would start. He kept looking round to the Jungle to see what the problem was, what he was doing wrong.

. . . at 3 a.m. I came across one of our boys fast asleep in a telephone kiosk . . .

SEAMUS MURPHY   For the Ajax match in 1982 the ferry was packed with Celtic supporters and the bar was drunk dry, the singing non-stop with flute accompaniment with volunteer solo spots – I got up and let fly with 'The Twenty-Fifth of May'. In Amsterdam we had a great time, meeting up with friends from London No 1 and Sunderland clubs – and we decided that win or lose we were going to have a good time. So none of us bothered to look for digs. Lots of fans spent the night in the canal boats; I just walked around; at 3 a.m. I came across one of our boys fast asleep in a telephone kiosk! Two seedy characters were about to lift his wallet. We woke the lad and went on to the station where more fans were sleeping, went aboard a train that was standing in the station, and had a kip before it was due out in the morning.

MICK MAHER   Amsterdam. On that occasion we went with a group from Heraghty's pub, a famous pub down in Allison

Street. There was a well-known character there called Charlie Devlin, a famous Celtic supporter – Peas and Barley, they called him. We all went with an overnight bag; Charlie's clothing for the trip was the sum total of what he was standing in, which was a pair of trousers, a Celtic blazer and a shirt and tie; and he had a passport, a toothbrush, six cans of Guinness and a bottle of vodka. That was it; the kit. We all got there at nine o'clock in the morning and the hotel wouldn't take us in, so we ended up visiting the Heineken Brewery – not a good way to start the day. And Charlie never actually got to the game – he fell asleep and didn't recover in time; he came home with his ticket in his pocket.

BRIAN CRAIG   Nightmare trips – one of the worst was the game in Cologne; when we had the massive scoreboard in the Mungesdorferstadion and after 23 minutes we could see 4–0 to them. Surprisingly enough, in the first half we thought we played quite well. But you know what the Germans are like on the break.

DOUGIE DICK   I wasn't there but a mate was telling us, that over in Cologne when we got beat 5–0 in 1982, the Rangers fans were all going mental as usual. This German police guy turns round to my mate big Gary and says, 'You lose 5–0 and you like this? I like to see you when you win!'

TOMMY HYNDMAN   One of the best European nights ever has got to be the Sporting Lisbon game. Celtic were trailing 2–0 from the first leg. Your man Burns was immense that night, Brian McClair – 2–0 at half-time, so that was them back level. And you just knew. At half-time you never even went for a pie. You just couldn't wait for them to come back on.

DAVIE HAY   Before the first leg against Notts Forest I got a call from two Scottish journalists who were already down in Nottingham. They said Brian Clough wanted me to go down to look at the ground because it was frosty; it let us see we had our correct footwear, it meant we could pre-warn the players about the conditions. So we were in Clough's room and there he was talking away. He happened to ask me what else I did and I said I had a pub, and of course if you say that to people you always say, like if you meet someone on holiday, 'Och, any time you're up in Scotland drop in and see me.' So we drew the first leg 0–0 down there. Before the second leg, we went down to Seamill on the Monday and I think on the Tuesday I got a call from my brother-in-law who was running the pub for me. 'Davie,' he says, 'Brian Clough's turned up in the pub. He says you promised him a drink.' And I said, 'Well, fine, give him a drink.' And he said, 'But he's got the whole team with him and he says Davie says the drinks are on him.' Clough had been clever enough to find out where it was, brought the bus along, brought the whole team in. What he had done, psychologically, was take the heat out of the game from his point of view. After all, there was going to be sixty-odd thousand there, a full house, people clamouring for tickets, a Scottish–English thing. It obviously worked; they beat us 2–1.

. . . See at night – they're like Jekyll and Hyde, the weans are trying to pick your pockets . . .

HARVEY BEATON The time we went to Porto and played that FC Porto, that was a nightmare. See the Portuguese people, they're lovely people – but see at night – they're like Jekyll and Hyde, the weans are trying to pick your pockets. And we're in this place, they called it The Cage. It was raining, at night, and they're all throwing these kung fu stars, and by the light of the floodlights you could see them all shining as they came over. So everybody had cushions all up. The next thing I see is this Rangers supporter talking to this guy, he must have asked this guy for a light. I don't know what the guy had in his mouth, but next thing it's like a flame-thrower – he must have had a mouth-ful of paraffin or something. After the game they held us behind for about 30 minutes, and there were kind of hummocks where they'd been doing some work on the ground, and this mob was standing there with bricks and bottles and all that. We'd to run the gauntlet to get out of there.

DANNY McGRAIN We didn't appreciate the travel properly. As a footballer you went east, west, north and south – in any direction, it didn't matter, because all you saw was the inside of hotels. As a young boy – 24, 25 – you're not interested enough in the culture of the country. It's only when you get to a stupid age like mine you appreciate it.

I remember when we went to the Acropolis in Greece – we were playing Olympiakos. We got to the gates – I think it cost 50 pence or a pound to get in. And Kenny Dalglish was sitting down; and I said, 'Are you going in?' Now I didn't know anything about the Acropolis, but I knew I should go in and see it, because it's been here a long, long time. But Kenny said, 'Och, it's a con.' I think he thought Wimpey had just built it – so he never came in. To us stupid, stupid boys it was just an old building; we'd rather be at the hotel having a swim. We went in; Kenny sat outside in the bus.

. . . at three o'clock in the morning we met these Italians who were out on a roundabout playing football . . .

ANDY ROBERTSON In 1984–85 we arrived in Milan and all the pubs were on strike and we couldn't get a drink. And everybody was out, hunting everywhere for a drink. At three o'clock in the morning we met these Italians who were out on a roundabout playing football. So we walked along and started playing with them and they all start shouting, 'Attila, Attila'. We're saying, 'Who the hell's Attila?' It was Big Mark Hateley – he was playing for them at that time. Next minute they all disappeared, then they came back with boxes of biscuits, bottles of wine, everything. Four o'clock in the morning, playing football with them, having a right bevvy.

JAMES DUNBAR The demise of playing in Europe is the biggest demotivating factor for the supporters. You looked forward to going abroad – that was how you gauged how good you were. You can win as many trophies as you like – but to gauge yourself against how good you are in the world, that's what's important.

The troubles in Ireland spread their sectarian poison into Scottish football in the mid-'80s when Old Firm teams made visits to Ireland.

FRANK GLENCROSS The worst experience of my life was coming back from the Celtic-Shamrock Rovers game in 1986. We were travelling in convoy, about 20 buses heading for the ferries at Larne at a quarter to one in the morning, and they were lying in the grass outside Belfast waiting for us. We were the first bus through, and we were lucky because they were just setting their sights when they hit us. But they hit every bus on the road and the last bus through was just a shambles; every window in it was broken. It was a well-rehearsed thing. The sectarian element, you know. Having said that there was provocation – on the way down the Celtic buses were hanging republican flags out the windows and what have you.

. . . in the second half Nicky Walker was too frightened to go near his goal because they were throwing darts at him . . .

DAVID McKINNON   We went to play Bohemians in Dublin – a crazy situation. We flew in to Dublin and had police escorts to the hotel, to the ground. We saw all the Gardai outside the ground; they felt that there was going to be a lot of trouble, because a lot of the fans had come down from the north. When we saw all the Gardai there and we were relieved; we waved to them. They gave us the V-sign back; so that wasn't very reassuring.

There was a huge fence around the park, and it was scary because it was half-dark as the floodlights weren't very good. I think there was a riot before the game but we played. I was running down the wing and I went into this fencing, and this guy came out of the darkness and and threw something at me like a huge rock; it hit the fence and bounced away.

There were people on the roofs with tricolours at the other end of the ground; I thought, 'All we need's a sniper now because it would make big news.' I think we drew 3–3 or lost 3–2; we were ahead, but in the second half Nicky Walker was frightened to go near his goal because they were throwing darts at him which were reaching the six-yard box, so he was out at the 18-yard line for the whole second half. If they got a corner darts were coming onto the pitch.

JOHN WATSON   Going to Dublin for the Bohemians game – that was wild. About '84, '85. It was my first time overseas, in Europe. I was about 16 or something; strolled over, ferry over to Dublin. Getting down towards the ground you could hear the Rangers fans everywhere, singing 'The Sash', 'Derry's Walls', everything, and it was building up to electric. The Bohemians fans were burning Union Jacks, tying them to the fence, and by the same token Rangers fans were burning Irish tricolours.

Behind the goal at the Rangers End there was a tower block and there were kids up on top of that throwing bricks, bottles, glasses, everything down. All they had to do was miss the road between the tower and the park, and – natural gravity – they were going to get this stuff in on top of us. The Rangers fans were going to the Gardai and asking them to move them off the tower-block, but ten minutes later this was still going on. So the Rangers fans started having a go at the Gardai; and eventually they retaliated. A big crowd from Northern Ireland went out and hammered the Gardai, coaxed them up a tunnel, got one of the big massive metal bins on them and took their shields and their batons off them.

After the game we strolled out – high, I was high, you know, it was like going to a war – and the Gardai were rattling the shields like in the film *Zulu*; and I remember just walking round and I was singing, thinking, 'This is the police, what are the police going to do?' Then I saw this guy, maybe 55, 60, some- body's granddad, not drunk, not causing trouble, in a shirt and tie and overcoat – he slightly stumbled towards the Gardai and whack – he got a baton to the side of the head. My mind went straight out of the party atmosphere. I was thinking, 'It's okay, the police can't do this . . .' But they did. I flew into the side of the wall and they just came right at us; they absolutely hammered us; the worst crowd I'd ever seen. They chased us back to the buses. At the buses there was a guy with a video camera – not like these wee cameras you get today – a right big thing. When the Gardai saw that they ran over and smashed it. They smashed the windows on our bus – if you were singing on the bus, they ran up and, f*** you, truncheons through the windows.

Then you'd a long journey home through the south. In Newry we got hit with petrol bombs, bottles, bricks, everything. It was a nightmare. It was the first time I've been glad to see the Strathclyde Police – they were policing Larne – 'Nice to see you, big man!'

Celtic also had a series of troubled evenings – not just a home and away, but a home, away and neutral ground tie against Rapid Vienna. Rangers–Bohemians at least had overtones which were historical or political; the Viennese whirl of pointless cheating and hooliganism seems now like a sign of the times as far as '80s football is concerned.

MURDO MacLEOD   I scored in the Vienna game. I think we lost 2–1 over there. We were behind anyway. At Celtic Park we played really well and we were 3–0 up when their player got 'hit' by an object. Whether it was a can or a coin or whatever, the boy went off and came back with a big bandage. They complained about it and it was one of these they'll-complain-but-nothing-will-be-done-about-it cases. Ninety-nine times out of 100 teams are asked to pay a fine but you're into the next round.

. . . he went by me like a breath of fresh air . . .

DANNY McGRAIN   The guy was never hit by the bottle; I think TV evidence showed that. The club thought we'd beat them once, we'll beat them again. But we beat them at Parkhead with the total backing of the crowd on a good night of football for us; taken away from our own support it just wasn't the same. We had attacked. I think we got a corner or something; the ball hit the crossbar and came out. I met their guy on the half-way line and he went by me like a breath of fresh air. I can't remember if he scored or if he passed to someone else to score.

ADAM SHIELS   That was one of our down nights, because two or three bampots went on to the pitch and attacked their goalkeeper.

STEVEN GALL   What soured it for the Celtic fans was that the guy who came onto the pitch at the end of the game and started kicking lumps out of Peter Pachult was based in London. You get these loonies from England. The guy was called James Honeyman, and he was sitting in the pub with us that night. He wasn't a genuine Celtic fan, just like the guys that did the slashings at Sunderland weren't genuine Rangers fans. On the journey coming home there was hardly a word uttered on the coach. Someone had a transistor on the coach – other people were going, 'Put that off!' We went home in silence – 64 people on the bus in silence.

DAVIE HAY We should have been in the quarter-finals, and who's to say how far we'd have gone? They went to the final and lost to Everton. As regards my problems as a manager – who knows what would have happened if that half-bottle of vodka hadn't been thrown?

SANDY STRANG The following Saturday these punters turned up – and there were about fourteen of them or so – in the enclosure facing the cameras at Ibrox and each of them had a letter – RAPID EXIT. There was a commercial at the time for Harp Lager – 'make a rapid exit'.

. . . the ballboys – they were the whole crowd . . .

MURDO MacLEOD After the Vienna game we had to play a closed-door game as a punishment. It was weird because you were playing one of the best sides in Europe – I think it was Atletico Madrid – and though it was at Parkhead it wasn't even as good as a training game. At a training game at least there's noise and there's a wee bit of banter, but this was one of the most important games of the season and there was no atmosphere, nothing there. The ballboys – they were the whole crowd.

Chapter Nine

TROUBLE

The late '70s and early '80s were grim times for football – a deep, dark decade. In recent years the fates of Scottish and English football have diverged; English supporters continue to disgrace themselves while Tartan Army foot-soldiers have become whiter than white. Back then, however, both Scottish and English football were heavily disrupted by spontaneous and organised violence.

In Scotland these troubled times were felt particularly keenly, since it accompanied the fall from world class in terms of what was happening on the pitch; in England teams whose supporters were running about Europe clubbing people were following winning teams, at least sometimes. This was a frustration easily as significant as the usually-cited political one, though the fact that seemingly endless rule by an apparently moral-free Conservative Party no doubt also contributed to the mood of discontent.

Before the '80s violence was mainly the clatter of drink-fuelled sore heads. Fans would go to games tanked up and get further tanked up during the game, so that by the time the referee gave the dubious penalty to the other side tempers were short and chances of trouble long. The post-1980 anti-booze at grounds legislation saw an end to all that and a change in the fundamental patterns of behaviour.

JOHN THOMSON   I found the crowds were much easier to deal with in the '40s than they are now. There wasn't the same element of evilness. At times you would get the odd hooligan element, but they were much more peaceful.

NEIL McDERMOTT Celtic–Rangers games I was not allowed to go to when I was a boy, for the simple reason that there was usually trouble; and, sad to say, the trouble was usually started by the Celtic supporters, since they were the poorer side at that time, in the '40s and '50s. They'd fall a couple of goals behind and then the supporters would have what they called a bottle party.

TOMMY HYNDMAN People at the back of the crowd would start throwing bottles. They were supposed to reach the park. They were supposed to go from the Celtic End to the Rangers End – so they were supposed to go maybe 200 yards to try and hit one of the opposition! And who was getting it? The kids at the front.

HUGH FERRIE I saw Celtic playing Milan – Inter Milan, when Dixie Deans missed a penalty. The crowds were always very calm – they used to accept defeats like that quite calmly. But with Old Firm matches it was different. I do remember coming back from one or two Celtic–Rangers games and saying to my daughter, 'Well, thank goodness we're out of that,' then turning the corner into Duke Street and running into a hail of stones. They actually pelted the cars with stones.

JOHNNY PATON At Old Firm games trouble wasn't a frequent thing, it was an occasional thing – depending on the circumstances and so on. The policemen would all be there and they'd be carrying them off by the dozen into the dressing-room and knocking them up against the wall. They knocked some sense into them in those days. Having said all that I was never scared or frightened; it never struck me. I never felt endangered. I don't think they were so violent and aggressive as this neo-Nazi crowd. In the '40s the supporters went to support their team and got carried away maybe – but football was what they were there for.

JIM COOKE When I was young, we would argue – it was a good goal or it wasn't a good goal, he should have done this or he shouldn't have done this – but there was no bad feeling. It all changed. It had changed even by the '70s. I remember one day down at Kilmarnock, I was in the enclosure. Rangers scored a goal and the Rangers support went to town. Kilmarnock scored; there were one or two Kilmarnock supporters near and they went to town. Kilmarnock scored a second one, and they went hysterical. This Rangers supporter got the Kilmarnock supporter by the back of the neck, and he said, 'Open your so-and-so mouth again and I'll close it.' So I turned round to him and I said, 'Look, mac, we go to town – it was a good goal – let him enjoy himself.' And he turned round to me and said, 'You open your mouth again and I'll shut it.' Before that, if I was in a crowd of opposing supporters, you could speak to them, say you were lucky, the usual thing you get at football – but now if I am going to Aberdeen, say, then even if I think it's a marvellous goal I won't open my mouth.

Glasgow crowds have always displayed a curious tendency for fighting amongst themselves.

JOHN LARKIN Celtic and Rangers fans have no tolerance whatsoever. I've seen players playing absolute crap, and they're calling him everything under the sun, and then the guy scores a goal and he's a hero and there's people saying, 'I told you so.' And they start arguing, 'I never called him that –' 'Yeah you did . . .' I've seen as many arguments among Celtic fans as I have with the opposition. I saw some really bad fights in the Celtic End years ago – the crowd used to just split, and you'd get people in the middle fighting.

JACK JARDINE You always got one in the crowd that disagreed with everybody. I did, in fact. I always liked Gerry Neef, for instance. Everybody hated Gerry Neef except me. I remember I was shouting for Gerry Neef and the guy next to me says, 'No wonder you're bald.' And Archie McArthur, next to me, he's going, 'That's it – Barlinnie for Christmas.'

The link between drink and all forms of trouble was indisputable. But for many years drinking and football were regarded by some as inseparable activities. The 1980 Act cut the cord.

JIM COOKE   The only time *we* took booze in was on New Year's Day, when you played the Celtic. At a New Year's game, the bottles were just passed along, back of you, in front of you. You just passed your bottle along – if it came back with something in it, good enough, if it didn't, well, so what? I would say they were the happiest years of support, because we were all of one mind. But you would see disturbances in other parts of the ground.

BRIAN CRAIG   I must admit I took in a couple of drinks myself. When it was allowed you used to see people going in with carry-outs. There were fights, and I must admit there were bottles flying when things weren't going so well; and obviously the vocal support was about a thousand decibels higher because anybody who's had a drink seems to want to sing.

GEORGE MOORE   I can go back a long time, and I liked a drink at the match. You'd get your wee carry-outs and stand together with your pals, just standing together, all the boys. Everybody would be steaming.

JOHN LARKIN   I saw this last year at Old Trafford, at the Mark Hughes testimonial; but I remember the same thing happening when there was no ban on drink. You'd see fans coming in, maybe four or five mates, and they'd be carrying another one in, drunk, and he'd sit on the stairs, and he wouldn't see any of the match. He'd be sitting unconscious on the stairs for the whole game. Then he'd suddenly wake up and go, 'WHAT'S THE SCORE?' You'd say, 'Aw, 2–1 mate.' And he'd go back to sleep, and about 15 minutes later he'd wake up again and say, 'WHAT'S THE SCORE?' Last summer, I was at the Man. United–Celtic game and this girl and her boyfriend came in. He was steaming and he sat for the whole game, seeing nothing. We were getting to the end of the game, everybody was quite tired, with just a couple of minutes to go, and he suddenly wakes up and he's jumping around and waving his flag about as if it's half an hour before the kick-off! Everyone else is practically asleep and he's bright as a button now, even though he's missed the whole game and he doesn't know what score it is. The game's finished and he's ready to start.

IAIN PATTERSON I think in the mid-'70s they changed the makeup of beer cans. I understand that in the early days you could throw them quite well; but then they changed them to a lighter alloy that sort of squashed so you couldn't throw them. The violence was mainly bottles and fists; in England it was knives, darts in the head. You didn't see stuff like that at Scottish games.

STEPHEN MURRAY I can remember before 1980 my dad used to stand me down at the front; and now and again, depending on what happened, people would throw bottles and they'd all rain down on the kids at the front. Where you had the drunks you had alcohol; where you had the alcohol you had bottles; where you had bottles you had violence.

TOMMY HYNDMAN The 1980 Scottish Cup final was a turning point. After that it became law that you couldn't have a drink at a game, and since then inside the ground it's been pretty much okay; though going and coming it's different – you get buses smashed, people attacked in the underground.

IAIN PATTERSON Sober fans – well, relatively sober fans – are less likely to go on the rampage than drunk fans. Fans can't take bottles and cans to the match and so they don't have the favourite weapons of the 1970s fans. But the re-designing of Ibrox into an all-seated stadium has also contributed; seats effectively act as barriers to pitch invasions. If you are seated anywhere apart from the first row you can't run through the seats to get on to the pitch and nobody in the front row is going to invade the pitch if they know that they will receive no support from the bulk of fans behind them.

HARVEY BEATON To me it's crazy – a double-edged sword. For all the hierarchy, there's that much drink up in the hospitality boxes; but the bears can't get any – don't give that to the scruffs, too bloody good for them. A law for one and a law for the other.

JACK JARDINE It's all booked up with businessmen, all doing business deals. Some of the crowds that go to Ibrox don't even see the game. They'll have an occasional watch at the game, then back to their lunch or their drink or whatever. They're allowed to drink all they want up there, but you can't drink if you're a punter.

STEF JARDINE What no drink at the game does is it makes everybody leave early to get to the pub. By the time the game's finished you're choking because you've had a drink before it. It's like a duty; you boo everybody going away. But you're saying to yourself, 'Christ, I wish I was going away with them.'

STUART DANIELS I drank at the game – I remember going in with a big carry-out. It was like an accordion going in, 24 cans of beer and a bottle of wine. I didn't want to throw any bottles – we just enjoyed ourselves. But I believe it's the best policy now, no alcohol, you can do without it. At one time I couldn't do without it – I can now.

DAVID PALMER The drink ban has made an enormous difference. I was very much in favour of banning alcohol and the police's powers to deny entry to any fan who appears to be drunk. I suppose putting back a load of pints provided some sort of sense of togetherness for the fans before they went to the match but you do have to balance that against some sense of social responsibility. People have died at matches, and when we set that against having a good time there isn't any comparison there.

The '80s brought a more sinister sort of violence altogether.

NEIL McDERMOTT I don't know exactly when the crowd turned really nasty. Generally it's to do with who's being successful. Usually the fault attributed to both sets of supporters is that Rangers fans are arrogant and Celtic fans suffer from paranoia. Rangers fans I would say are definitely arrogant when they are on top, and I think possibly the '80s bred that kind of behaviour – maybe it was a reflection of society. I don't want to be too political but, with the kind of government of the time, the idea that success was everything. . . it was not a matter of playing football to enjoy it, or going along to watch – they had to win. It turned the whole atmosphere sour.

JOE SHEVLIN   You got these groups getting together – the Casuals. They came up with the big boots on, the spiky haircuts. The police always ignored these ones and went for the boys that weren't going to give any trouble; they turned a blind eye to the neds.

IAIN PATTERSON   In the 1980s there was supposedly an Inter-City Firm, a small group of Rangers Casuals. I don't think they amounted to much. In Scottish terms the clubs with the biggest Casual support were Aberdeen, Motherwell and Hibernian. I've no idea why the Casuals never took off at Ibrox. They weren't liked by the mass of supporters; they tended to be a different generation from the 1970s rioters; then rioting was more spontaneous.

JOHN WATSON   The early '80s, when you had the Hibs Casuals, the Inter-City Firms and so on – that was when the Casuals were big in Scotland. Rangers never had a big squad then – there were maybe three hundred. For the size of the Rangers support that wasn't many. We always treated ours like young kids – three hundred young kids running around. You'd think, 'What a bunch of wankers.' It's like these boys now who run about with mobile phones. I laugh at this – you phone up a guy you're going to fight? Can you ring someone up, say, 'Meet you at nine o'clock,' turn up, then slash them? And then meet up the following week and say, 'That was some fight we had last week!' What's the mentality?

They're just thugs. I've been in fights loads of times with Celtic fans. That's because of their team, maybe because of their religion, maybe because they're supporting the likes of Adams and I'm a loyalist. But there are times and places for that. I'm not going about with a bunch of Casuals to have a street-fight for the sake of it.

STEVEN GALL   They were from different parts of Glasgow – Castlemilk, Drumchapel, Springburn, Easterhouse – and they kind of formed themself into gangs – they wanted to go back to the gang-fight days of the early to late '60s. They would arrange a meeting-point to have a fight, and in the meantime get warmed up by having a fight amongst themselves!

TOMMY HYNDMAN   Daft wee boys of about 14 thinking they were hard men. But the crowd that were the true Celtic support, the guys in their twenties, they'd get a grip of them and be giving them a slap round the ear or a kick up the backside and telling them to get to buggery, because they'd nothing to do with Celtic. The real supporters went and tore into them, gave them a right good smacking before the police or the opposition supporters could get there. They didn't want the name of their club besmirched by the likes of scum like that.

One result of this era – though the idea of segregation goes back much further than the '80s – was a more intense police presence.

ADAM SHIELS   One thing I don't like about the football nowadays is the change from the '60s; in the '60s we went – at the start anyway – and you all stood in one big crowd – you weren't segregated, with Celtic supporters there, Motherwell supporters at the other end – you were all next to each other, and the crack was good – you were talking away and getting different bits of patter.

NEIL McDERMOTT   Things seemed to get worse as the years went by – you got almost complete segregation. Now it's absurd – you get Aberdeen, Hearts, even Partick Thistle supporters segregated at Parkhead and Ibrox.

JOHN LARKIN   Nowadays you never see an opposition fan until you're in the ground. If they changed the segregation now – they'd find out that nothing had changed. If anything, it's probably worse. People don't know how to stand – or sit – together any more.

JIMMY FINNIS   What's actually happened has been for the better, in a way. I know that all the changes aren't good, but you can just about go to the games without any risk now. I remember back in the old days, you used to have all sorts of sporadic trouble; you'd have maybe Celtic fans on one side of the road, walking down to Easter Road; and Hibs fans on the other. And a few songs would start; the police would be walking down the middle. And then some daft wee boy would try to run across and there'd be a wee exchange. It was like antelopes, you know, locking horns. But drink did make people get carried away. What's happened now is that supporters are interested in controlling themselves. So when the boys go abroad, maybe, say with Scotland – you have older guys there who are controlling them and making sure that they don't go over the top. They're all steaming; but they're under control. So they have a good time, but the football's first. That's the big change. For a while back then in the '80s, there were people who were there for the fight and the football was just incidental. Now we're back where we were before; there may be trouble, but it's temper, not timetabled.

Chapter Ten

REVOLUTIONS
1985–1995

The years between 1985 and 1995 saw revolutions at Celtic Park and at Ibrox. At Celtic Park a period of relative success was followed by intense discontent and, finally, blood-letting – only by the end of the century, perhaps, shall we see what has been achieved at the price of the blood on the boardroom floor. Rangers managed their revolution in a more velvet-gloved way. What Rangers became in the late '80s was unrecognisable from the shambolic organisation that was playing to half-empty houses during Jock Wallace's second spell as manager. The change was brought about by the ambitious appointment of Graeme Souness who, with the help of huge sums of money, transformed Rangers as utterly as Stein did Celtic in the '60s. Even in his passing on are the effects of his presence felt. Celtic can only hope that their revolution, partly powered by embarrassment at Ibrox successes, will be half as successful.

STUART DANIELS   He ruffled a few feathers, Souness, but he was good for the Scottish game.

DAVID McKINNON   The players knew that there had to be changes; the club was moving up a gear. Souness came to the first day's training; he'd just flown in from Majorca. Now there was always a tradition at Rangers that you had to wear tie-ups with your socks up at training, you had to come in wearing a suit and tie, you couldn't have a moustache or a beard. Souness turns up casual – open neck shirt, moustache, socks round his ankles. Somebody tackled him at training and he had a gash; it all went quiet, everybody trying to work out what he would do, how he was going to react. Next thing, there was a 50-50 ball and he did the guy that tackled him.

. . . he stood on the ball before arrogantly flicking it away . . .

IAIN PATTERSON When Souness came there was great excitement. The weekend before there was talk in the papers that he was going to manage Spurs or Arsenal. But I was excited rather than pleased. Souness had been booed on many occasions by the Scotland supporters, and I don't think many people liked him. On the other hand he was a winner.

Rangers have got an arrogant support; we like arrogant players, gallus players, players who strut about and let people know that they are inferior. People thought that Souness was out of the Rangers tradition when he first arrived, but in terms of arrogance he was central. If you ask most Rangers fans what Graeme Souness's greatest moment as an Ibrox player was they would tell you about the New Year game against Celtic in his first season. During the first half he got the ball on the half-way line; he controlled it; he swayed one way and sent Celtic players another; and he stood on the ball before arrogantly flicking it away. It didn't lead to a goal – it wasn't important or crucial in terms of the match – it was just a cameo moment and I think the Rangers fans just loved it. You don't do that because it adds anything to the game – you do these things to humiliate the opposition.

JOHN WATSON Davie Cooper would run towards the Jungle, whereas other folk would run away from it – just to annoy *them*. Souness was the same – he'd come out and warm up right in front of them – stretch and that, right in front of the Jungle. The guy's a millionaire, he's no need to do that. Gallus.

JIMMY NICHOLL   Souness was a bit of a mystery. It was only when I went on the staff towards the end of my time at Ibrox that I used to see the other side of him. He used to be great from 9.30 to 10.30 in the morning, having a cup of tea, he and Walter Smith telling stories and talking football. Then the mask came on; from 10.30 to 12.00, the training, I think he found it hard to be as light-hearted. To the players he would say, 'Live right and do things properly; your career finishes just like that.' But it's hard in Scotland to do what he was saying; you look at Iain Durrant. He lived round the corner from Ibrox and if his mates came to the door and asked him to come for a drink and if he said no then he got slaughtered – 'so we're not good enough for you' – and if he went out he got slaughtered. In that first season everything went well in the end; we won the title. But it started with the Hibs game. George McCluskey had a horren-dous injury and Souness was off – it wasn't the best of starts.

GEORGE McLEOD   A sign of how things had changed, that one against Hibs. The season before you could have got into almost any game except the Old Firm game, cash on the gate. I drove through to Edinburgh and found it was all-ticket only when I got there. I ended up walking about the ground, because the atmosphere was so special; and when Souness got sent off – what a noise from the Hibs fans. Sheer glee. The earth shook. It was the start of that joke – Celtic fans going into pubs and asking for a Souness – a Souness being 'one half and I'm off'.

TERRY BUTCHER   The first game against Hibs was when Souness got sent off and it was a mass brawl; we started off completely the wrong way. Then we beat Falkirk at home 1–0; the crowd expected us to beat them by more. Then we lost at home to Dundee United 3–2, after being 2–0 up at half-time. It was a disastrous start. Then we started to pick up rhythm and win games; we took the League Cup, beat Celtic and took off from there. We finally won the League at Aberdeen; I scored and we drew 1–1. Souness got sent off again.

COLIN LAMOND   That year I didn't actually get to the title-winning game at Pittodrie. My brother went, and he said it was the biggest sense of relief. I suppose it was the same sort of relief

that Celtic felt when they came back after the period of no
trophies that they'd been having. It was huge – we'd got our
team back from the dead.

Souness set about his business briskly. Over his years in
charge he made a series of signings that made Rangers fans in
turn delighted, vexed and outraged. First Englishmen, then
blacks, then – in the face of a century of tradition – a Catholic
player arrived at Ibrox. The first arrivals were less controversial,
though controversy did follow them in due course.

GORDON INGLIS   The fans loved the fact that the trend of
the best Scottish players going south to England had been
reversed, and we bought in at one fell swoop the English team
captain, Terry Butcher, the best goalkeeper in the country, Chris
Woods, and one of the most stalwart defenders in the country,
Graham Roberts.

. . . I really wanted to go to Manchester United . . .

TERRY BUTCHER   I had to be sold the move; I was of the
opinion that Scottish football was a Mickey Mouse league and it
was really no place to go. I really wanted to go to Manchester
United. Souness brought me up here and I got the trophy room
tour and in the end it was great. It was amazing, the attention we
got; being in Glasgow was like being in Italy, with fans paying
attention to your every move and so on. In Bridge of Allan it was
like Beverly Hills, like the tours that go past the houses of the
Beverly Hills movie stars. Up on the hill in Bridge of Allan you
got people coming up with cars, cruising past the gates and
having a look in. Some would get out and take pictures and
everything else, and then off they'd go. We were treated like
gods.

  When we did lose games I'd come off and I would feel angry
and I would kick things and throw things and I'd bang doors.
And the Rangers public would like that because I was somebody
that felt like them. Once it was in public; I didn't know what I'd
done, that it was live on television. We'd been beaten 1–0 by
Aberdeen and Billy McNeill was being interviewed. I was

coming up the steps and some ladies said something and I just flung open one of these doors; it just crashed open. Billy McNeill turned round as if there was a fight or something; I just stormed past him, and he said, 'As you can see, the Rangers players aren't very happy.'

IAIN PATTERSON The crowd took to them, especially Graham Roberts. He was a hard player and they genuinely like hard players. He was a bit of a personality, and he gave the impression that he was on the fans' side. Conducting the crowd helped him a bit, of course.

STUART DANIELS I don't think Roberts completely understood the religious emphasis – I dare say he and Butcher were a bit naïve on that score. They didn't realise what the West of Scotland thing really meant.

. . . if you're going up to Larkhall, just say "No Surrender" . . .

ANDY ROBERTSON I had Graham Roberts up at the Supporters' Club dance and I asked him his greatest moments in football; he said, winning the UEFA Cup with Spurs and Rangers drawing 2–2 with Celtic with nine men. That was the day he mimed playing the orange flute. At Terry Butcher's first-ever dance, he made a statement. He said, 'It's great to be up in Scotland,' he said, 'and the first thing I got told when I signed with Rangers was, if you're going up to Larkhall just say "No Surrender". That's what he said on stage, 'No Surrender' – everybody went daft.

This acquired passion led Butcher and the others not only into trouble, but into court.

COLIN LAMOND The Breach of the Peace case was in the 1987–88 season. That was some incident. Those guys had become Rangers-daft – Rangers supporters as well as Rangers players, especially Graham Roberts.

NEIL McDERMOTT I remember thinking when Souness arrived and he started bringing in English players that this would make things more civilised. Amazingly it had the opposite effect. Four of them landed in court after we'd had McAvennie of Celtic – biased account this one – almost being mugged by Chris Woods, Terry Butcher and Graham Roberts. All Englishmen. This astonished me – I thought they would have brought some sanity to the scene. But maybe they were trying to prove they were more Scottish than the Scots when it came to the fire and fervour of an Old Firm game. More loyal than the loyalists. The charitable interpretation was that they didn't understand. I think they did.

COLIN GLASS Do you recall the Old Firm game in 1987 when the police got called in? I was actually sitting in the directors' box that day. I'd been invited. I remember sitting there thinking, 'This is the directors' box, just behave yourself, there's guests here, just sit down there and applaud politely, don't get carried away.' But when Gough scored the equaliser, when Rangers were down to nine men, I was going mad. But no one would have noticed, because the directors' box was going like the Copland Road stand.

Mark Walters was the first black player to wear Rangers' colours. As an out-and-out winger he was warmly received by Rangers' fans. But Walters found the rest of Scotland primitive in its racial attitudes.

MARK DINGWALL A lot more has been made of Walters since he left than when he came. The big taboo at Ibrox was never the colour of your skin; it was the religion that mattered. People loved Walters because of his skill. Also, it was a case of inverted snobbery, because he was *our* black player.

IAIN PATTERSON Mark Walters' first game was against Celtic away. The crowd were positive because he was a winger and he looked good. First against Celtic but primarily against Hearts the following week he was bombarded with bananas; it sort of reinforced the Rangers fans. It made the front page of the *Daily Record* when someone made a racist chant and they took away his season ticket. I suppose if we were being honest – if Celtic had signed a black player before us then the Rangers fans would have booed him.

Rangers' fans were less enthusiastic about Souness's next major signing, Maurice Johnston. Johnston was not only a Catholic but West of Scotland Catholic; he was an ex-Celtic player guilty of sundry anti-Rangers offences; he was a player apparently on the verge of returning to Parkhead. In other words, he offered plenty of get-out clauses which allowed the Ibrox diehards who opposed the signing to protest that their objections had nothing to do with religion.

The signing was the end of an era. Over the years Rangers fans had continued to support a system which offered no surrender not so much to the IRA, as the song goes, but to the civilised world. A pattern of bigotry at the heart of one of Scotland's greatest and most powerful institutions was broken. Whatever his motives, Souness displayed a courage which assures him of a certain historical position which none of his other achievements can match.

As far as Mojo is concerned – he was, for a time, Christendom's answer to Salman Rushdie. At least Salman Rushdie had only one side after him. But many of the Rangers faithful were soon converted, not least because the signing caused so much discomfiture to their rivals.

TOMMY HYNDMAN Judas Johnston. He phoned Dial-a-Prayer and they hung up on him. He phoned them again and they sent him ten bob for the gas.

RICHARD GOUGH I learnt about it when we were away; we were flying out to our usual pre-season training camp, and Graeme Souness told me, 'Oh, by the way we are signing a friend of yours – Maurice Johnston.' And I'm thinking, 'Johnston, yeah right, good one Graeme.' To most of the players what Maurice was or wasn't didn't mean much; at that time McCoist and myself were the only Scottish ones playing in the team. Most of the boys were English and it didn't mean much to them.

STUART DANIELS   When he first signed, I didn't like it. I've got to be honest. That day I met my wee mate Adam Malcolm – Rangers-daft. He said, 'What do you think, big man?' I said, 'Sad news.' It wasn't so much that he was a Roman Catholic, it was what he'd done before that, who he'd played for. He'd made the sign of the cross, he'd butted Stuart Munro in a Cup final at Hampden. It was the individual, not his religion.

It broke my brother's heart – he fell out with me. He said, 'It's a good job your father's dead, he'd kill you going to see Rangers now.' He kept away, my older brother, for that time. (In fact, if the truth be known, he sneaked up to one game, at Parkhead in the Scottish Cup, sneaked up incognito, his anorak over his head.)

A lot of the guys down at Ibrox that day were level-headed; one said to me, 'Stuart, give this time, he'll be a good signing for us'; but there were a couple of guys down there who were badly affected. One fellow arrived in a hard hat; he was on the television. He says, 'All right, Stuart? – I've lost my f***ing job because of this. I was getting kidded on in The Bothy, Maurice Johnston's signed for Rangers, all my workmates were kidding me on, I couldn't stand it – I told the gaffer to stick the job up his arse.' There were two guys arrived with a wreath; they burned their season books and laid a wreath outside Ibrox.

That day I waited till Souness came out. Souness crossed the road over to his car. I said, 'Graeme, do you realise what you've f***ing done?' He looked at me; he'd seen me before so he knew I hadn't just landed in a parachute; he knew that more or less the Rangers were my life. And he said, 'Give it six months, big man, and get back to me on it.' That was in July, the tenth of July. And I went down at Christmas time, and I was in the foyer, and he says, 'OK?' I says, 'Can I have a word with you, Graeme?' I says, 'I owe you an apology.' He says, 'I told you, didn't I? The wee man's the business.'

It became a fun thing; I used it in our favour. Staying in the Gorbals – it's a high Celtic area – there's people coming up to me and saying, 'Stuart – Maurice Johnston – you'll no like that.' And I said to myself, 'I'm programmed here to say, no, I'm finished, I'm no going back to see Rangers now, that's it, Fenian bastard, Roman Catholic, whatever.' But I never. I said, 'It's great, I love it.' I saw them taken aback with it, and I said, 'We're going to get your captain off you!' That was Paul McStay, who I don't rate at all, by the way – Mr Personality-Minus, I wouldn't have him on top of the mantelpiece – but I'd say, 'We're going to get your captain off you.' So I used it to our advantage. I think some people did stop going; but I think a lot went back while he was there. I think a lot changed at 4.38 p.m. on November the fourth 1989 when he scored the winner against Celtic at Ibrox. I think that's when he got accepted by the doubters.

. . . it's the shekels that count; religion doesn't keep you . . .

JACK PRIOR   To me he was just a restless wee player. He's a brave man, but it's the shekels that count; religion doesn't keep you. When he scored that last-minute goal, he turned round, looked at the Celtic fans, then ran . . .

IAIN PATTERSON   I suspect that most of the Rangers supporters tolerated rather than rejoiced in Johnston's presence in the team. I can remember a game against Dunfermline in 1990. Part of the East Enclosure was singing 'Mo, Mo, Super Mo, Super Maurice Johnston', while another section was singing, 'Mo, Mo, F*** Your Mo, F*** Your Maurice Johnston.' I suspect that few shed many tears when the news came through that he had been shipped off to Everton. The story goes – probably apocryphal – that the day of his departure witnessed the largest number of enquiries about The Rangers Bond received by the club on any one day.

GORDON INGLIS   Mo Johnston remains the one huge doubt in the minds of Rangers fans. I think nowadays there is a far more mature outlook regarding what a player means to the club – they'll look at the player's skill first, not his religion. You've now got the first black Catholic at Ibrox in Basile Boli. Nobody really considers his Catholicism at all.

HARVEY BEATON   I saw Boli playing for Marseille and I thought, 'What a player – they'll all be putting sick-lines in when they've to play him.' You had the press again: 'Rangers have signed a Catholic.' I support Rangers; he's a Rangers player; I couldn't give a f*** if he's a Martian.

Rangers had taken over at home under a man who, like Stein, saw that winning what the domestic game had to offer was not enough. But Souness, apart from a couple of individual matches, had no European triumphs which would have convinced the doubters that he was a great manager; and Celtic supporters still refused to have Lisbon smiles rubbed off their faces.

STEVEN GALL   A few seasons ago we had the red stars on the terraces. Rangers had just got beat by Red Star Belgrade – the cards had a white three on a red background. It was Graeme Souness's quote – 'Judge me on my European record' – and we were saying, played three, lost three, something like that.

TERRY BUTCHER   We didn't have a lot of success abroad. We played Gornik in the European Cup; we won 3–1 at home. It's a funny lead in European football, 3–1; we went out there and we stayed near Krakow, right near Auschwitz. There was such a strange atmosphere; Poland was such a miserable, grey place. We lost to Steaua Bucharest after.

ROBERT MALCOLM   Bucharest was a real culture shock. Ceausescu was still in charge. The place was like Glasgow city centre on a Saturday afternoon until it came to six o'clock at night and nothing moved – there was a curfew. We stayed in a hotel which had the only disco in Bucharest – and they closed it for the night we were there.

BRIAN CRAIG   The worst place I've ever been was Romania. Everybody's head was down about their ankles. Maybe it's brightened up a bit since Ceausescu's gone – but the people – it was the living dead over there.

DOUGIE DICK   The Secret Police were following us every-where – we almost got arrested for crossing the road without the green man! We wouldn't wait for anything green. In the ground, you looked about and thought, 'There's nobody here!' Their fans were all army; army right round. It wasn't ordinary punters, it was just the army all in green coats. Fifteen hundred Rangers there, all singing the American national anthem just to noise off the communists.

RICHARD GOUGH It was disappointing to go out in Europe; all I can say which justifies us is that we came up against teams that went on to the finals. We played Munich, we played Bucharest, we played Red Star Belgrade. They were quality teams; we weren't put out by the sort of team we've been going out to latterly – the AEKs and the Levskis.

Souness gained one big scalp – Dynamo Kiev, aka the Russian national team, defeated on a night of unusual passion, and of even more unusual line-painting – at Ibrox.

JIMMY NICHOLL The Kiev one was a cracker; it was when Souness brought the pitch in so they wouldn't have the width of the whole pitch to turn and switch players and get in between our full-backs and centre-halves. I remember vividly, early in the game – the outside-left, a diagonal ball comes from the right hand side of the park – a great switch, counter-attacking. The outside-left controlled the ball on his chest, head down, and he's going to take me on – and he was already over the white line! I just casually walked up and let him run past me.

GORDON INGLIS The Dynamo Kiev match – again Rangers were a goal down from the first leg and scored two at Ibrox to go through. And I remember, for the last 25 minutes of the match, the crowd were continually on a roar, which I'd never experienced before.

. . . Ally McCoist did one of the best misheaders of all time . . .

TERRY BUTCHER I'll never forget that game. The atmosphere when we equalised was unbelievable; the crowd was singing and everything. We scored to make it 2–0 when Ally McCoist did one of the best misheaders of all time and completely foxed the Kiev keeper. When that went in I thought the roof was going to come down; the hairs on the back of your neck were standing up; it gives me goose bumps thinking about it.

Souness moved on after a few years; but he left behind an immensely changed organisation. One effect of the Souness changes was making Ibrox a lot more open for business. The late '80s saw an increase in commercialism on a grand scale. Amongst some fans there is a realisation that the regime now led by metals tycoon David Murray may bring European success; others see a game and a club drifting inevitably away from its roots, from the bedrock of its support amongst working people, floating on a tide of bond schemes and corporate hospitality.

GORDON INGLIS Rangers is big business. Now the club is geared to success; success allows it to exploit its business potential to the full. There's a whole range of corporate arrangements that have only come about since we had a successful team on the park. It's a vicious circle: if you have a successful team then it's easy to encourage business ventures; if you have big business ventures then you can pay for a better team.

BRIAN CRAIG The character of the support has changed, what with the commercial aspects, with the executive boxes, with the Club Deck. A lot of people say, 'Where were they at the Partick Thistle game at Ibrox – after the 4–2 game – when there were only 2,000?' They say, 'If we hit another disaster, where will the camel coats be?'

COLIN GLASS As a bond holder I don't feel different. The fans around my bond seat are different from the people I stood next to on the terraces in the '70s. There are more older people, though many of them have a bond seat for their child. There'd be quite a few who would have been standing beside me in the '70s and who have now progressed in their careers. They're not so fanatical as the fans who populated the East Enclosure; but they're not poseurs or part of what's known as the camel-coat brigade; they've a deep, deep love of football and of Rangers.

. . . you were seeing women who looked like they'd stepped out of Ascot . . .

MARK DINGWALL   The only time I could personally say I've noticed a difference was the Leeds game and the Marseille game in the Champions' League, when I had tickets for the Club Deck. Against Leeds and against Marseille you were seeing women up there who looked like they'd stepped out of Ascot – it was very obvious they'd been brought along by guests or hubby or whatever.

JACK JARDINE   It's all season tickets and I haven't got a season ticket. If I take a notion – maybe there's a game, Rangers are playing somebody and I say to myself, 'I wouldn't mind seeing that,' there's no chance. Eventually they're going to lose the support with all this; or it's just going to be a crowd of business-men doing their deals and whatnot. There's only going to be one sort of class – the working class are going to finish up pushed out.

BILL LAMOND   The boys aren't disappearing – when you consider that a kid will pay £80 for a pair of trainers – going to Ibrox on a Saturday is no big deal. I saw one young mother at Ibrox at the six-in-a-row game – two youngsters, eight years of age, ten years of age – both had the full strip on, the full rig-out, you're maybe talking about £80 – this mother had obviously spent eighty quid on a full rigout for the two kids to go to the League flag day. It's no big deal as far as cash goes.

JACK JARDINE   We've got the money to weaken you and strengthen us. Where's the glory in that? Mikhailichenko – I was calling him Michelangelo for ages – you don't even know the players' names, never mind anything else. How can you really put yourself to have real sympathy with them? You get players who say they're desperate to play for Rangers. It's funny how they're all desperate to play for Rangers until they leave – 'Oh, Rangers, the only team for me . . .' – and then they're off.

185

Obviously they're going to say they're Rangers daft while they're at Rangers – 'This has been my dream . . .' What a load of baloney!

You're not allowed to throw a wee blue label as you were in my day, or pee in somebody's pocket . . .

ALEX MacDONALD   I'm not so sure if all the singing and dancing is as good now as it was way back. You're not allowed to throw a wee blue label, as you were in my days, or pee in somebody's pocket. It's all hoity-toity now, cigars and pakora and things like that. In the old days if you didn't like a player it was hit him with a pie; you miss all that. You miss the Tradeston thing; we walked along past Paisley Road Toll; there were tenements there and everybody was just glad to get along to Ibrox and get singing. Now they're coming from four bedrooms.

STUART DANIELS   Traditional Rangers fans, working-class supporters might lose out. If Mr Murray and Steven Spielberg and Paul McCartney and Donald Trump go for a pint of lager and it's £50 for a pint of lager, it's not a problem for them, but it's a problem for Stuart Daniels, who's unemployed and gets £187 a fortnight to keep a wife and a family. But maybe it's a price worth paying. You only get in life what you pay for, and maybe it's a price worth paying if Rangers can win the European Cup.

A more realistic target for Rangers was the avenging of the 7–1 defeat by Celtic of 1957. In 1988 they came close to matching that mythical scoreline.

Any time that I'm depressed and down, I get the 5–1 game on the video and that fair perks me up . . .

HARVEY BEATON   The 5–1 game, when Ray Wilkins scored – see any time that I'm depressed and down, I get the 5–1 game on the video and that fair perks me up. The wife'll say, 'Have you got that f***ing 5–1 video on again?' – I tell you, it's better than a drug. I get my Rangers tapes on – I always put them on when she's out. Any time you're down and blue, who needs valium? I just get the tapes on.

BRIAN CRAIG   The 5–1 game was an incredible game. Ally McCoist said after that we should have gone for the throat, because the 7–1 game will stick with us. But we took the foot off the pedal. So no complaints with five; but slight regrets – we should have gone for eight.

ALEX BELL   I'd gone to get a Rangers calendar for my son; I had it in a Rangers bag from the club shop. And as I was coming up by the main stand I was saying, 'We're awful close to the Celtic End, wherever we are . . .' So I said to a steward, 'I don't think my ticket's for the right place. I'm a Rangers supporter up from London . . .' He says, 'Sorry, I can't do a thing about it.' So I went into the Gents' and stuffed the calendar down the back of my trousers, and sat down. I said to my wife, 'I feel a bit uncomfortable being here.' She said, 'Do you want to leave?' I said, 'Well, we'll see how it goes.' And Celtic scored in the first minutes; all the Celtic fans stood up so we stood up as well; and I'm wanting to go, but we stayed. And Rangers equalised. We just sat there; the whole end was in silence and my wife and I just sat there; we sort of nudged each other, and that was the only thing that moved. A couple of minutes later Wilkins hit this screamer; again we nudged each other; again, the only thing that moved in that whole end. At half-time my wife – she's a Londoner, a Spurs fan – said, 'I thought it was just you lot that were daft; now I realise you're both just as bad as the other in the biasedness.' The thing that amazed her was that she was sitting amongst people who were really quite well-dressed; Rolex watches and things like that; and they're all screaming abuse. Finally at half-time I saw the same man at the barricade; and I told him a lie; I said, 'They've been abusing my wife.' He said, 'All right.' He spoke into the microphone and the next thing the gate was opened and we moved through into the other side and got a couple of seats there. Rangers won 5–1. I don't know whether I could have sat through the whole 90 minutes even with five going in. It wasn't even as if the Celtic End would have been deserted; both teams were going through this funny time when they were trying to outdo each other in demonstrating their loyalty.

Celtic's Cup win in 1989 gave Rangers supporters an opportunity to do just that.

MARK DINGWALL   Strangely, one of the best memories is of a defeat, in the 1989 Scottish Cup final, when Celtic beat us 1–0. After the game, about half the Rangers End stayed. We just stood, and sang, and chanted and whatever, until the Celtic End was empty. And just that feeling of being with people who cared enough to stay, and celebrate our team even in defeat – that was one of the best things.

JOHN WATSON   The best thing about that game was when I went home. Now you don't buy papers for two days let alone watch a video after a game if you've lost, but eventually I watched this video. And after Celtic have got the Cup the commentator's right down at the Celtic End, and he says to big Aitken, 'It must be some feeling winning the Cup, stopping Rangers winning the Treble,' and big Roy says, 'Oh brilliant – look what it means to these fans – listen to what it means to these fans . . .' And he stops to listen. But all you can hear is 'The Billy Boys'. The Celtic fans have got their mouths open, but all you hear is 'Follow, Follow. . .' Brilliant. Twenty years on somebody's going to sit down to watch that and he'll have to listen to us!

TOMMY HYNDMAN   We Celtic fans had all these mad T-shirts printed with Bart Simpson pulling his shorts off, and 'Treble My Arse' on them.

The early part of the 1985–95 decade carried little suggestion of how dire the rest of it would be for Celtic. They took the title in dramatic circumstances in 1986 and then again in 1988, breaking into Souness's initial run of success. The Cup was won in the Centenary Year – 1988 – and held on to in 1989. After that it has been mainly gloom and doom – until May 27th,

1995, anyway – internal wranglings, boardroom coups, managerial departures, supporter discontent and Raith Rovers.

Davie Hay was manager for the 1986 campaign when Hearts – always the bridesmaids – were beaten to the finish; Billy McNeill had returned by the 1988 Double Season.

DAVIE HAY   On the last day we had to go to Love Street and win well, I think by three or four; but even then Hearts had only to get a point at Dundee.

DANNY McGRAIN   When we played St Mirren at Love Street, the crowd was buzzing. All those wee transistors at people's ears.

DAVIE HAY   What was lost that day was how well Celtic played in the first half. I think that there were people who were spreading the rumour at half-time that Hearts were losing; we were winning 4–0 and so there was a false hope and then a disappointment. Then there were two goals at Dens in the space of a few minutes. The place was just bedlam.

Albert Kidd was a Celtic fan through and through . . .

TOMMY HYNDMAN   Albert Kidd scored twice for Dundee. The Hearts fans couldn't believe it; he was going mental, even though Dundee were getting relegated anyway, because Albert Kidd was a Celtic fan through and through. The Hearts fans threw their scarves away, and Albert Kidd was the guest of honour at a lot of Celtic dances that year. The Hibs Player of the Year too, was he?

STEVEN GALL   Winning the League at Paisley after chasing Hearts for the whole long, weary road – that was a high point. I remember coming out of games that season, and asking, 'How did Hearts get on the day?' 'They won again, they won again.' It was a case of, 'How are we going to claw this outfit back?' They went up to Dundee, we went to Paisley . . . a day for the transistors. The supporters' buses didn't leave Paisley for many an hour.

MICK McCARTHY We had a good squad of players in 1988. Packy Bonner, Roy Aitken, Derek Whyte, Peter Grant; I had more fights with Granty than anybody; even though we were on the same team, even though we roomed together. He played for the jersey, even in training games. Frank McAvennie; at that time he was courting a girl in London and he spent half his time in London and half in Glasgow. The players were going to club together and fly him straight from London to the training ground.

MURDO MacLEOD Winning things in special seasons is something that seems to be destined for Celtic – like in the Centenary year, when they won the Double.

STEVEN GALL That season several times we were maybe nothing-each with five, four, three minutes to go. But we always knew that there was a goal there, especially in the Cup semi-final against Hearts. I remember at the semi-final, the announcer came over the tannoy with something like five minutes to go saying, 'Extra-time will be played' – and a huge cry came up from the Celtic supporters – 'We don't need extra-time!' And Mark McGhee scored.

MICK MAHER I came back from New Zealand for two months in the Centenary year – from St Patrick's Day until the Cup final. I went to see Celtic–Motherwell at Fir Park with some friends of mine and I timed Anton Rogan's winning goal at 44 minutes 59 seconds of the second half.

TOMMY HYNDMAN There used to be a wee enclosure at Hampden in front of the main stand – we were in there that day, the day of the Centenary Cup final. Celtic were 1–0 down with about ten minutes to go. My brother James – he was about fourteen – was standing next to me greeting, bawling his eyes out. I went, 'Don't panic – we're going to win this.' In those days, people were going with five minutes to go, 'Don't leave, we're going to score.' And sure enough, we got the two goals. The whole place went mental.

JAMES DUNBAR   Standing at Hampden with my best mate – we used to go to all the games together – with the tears running down the face . . . That's my happiest memory.

Centenary Year memories are all Celts had to hold on to to keep them warm during a period of poor results that lasted from 1989 to 1995. There have been distractions off the field, though.

JACK PRIOR   I was up at Parkhead getting my photos taken. A quiet morning. The clown who was showing us round says, 'Come on and I'll show you the trophy rooms.' I says, 'Do you mean the antique rooms?'

BRIAN McBRIDE   It was quite tough being a Celtic fan in the early '90s; in fact we got the same jokes made about us that we used to make about Partick Thistle. Even the English, who always remember the Partick Thistle jokes, were using Celtic jokes in their place.

Distraction number 1: the replacement of the solid feet-under-the-table managerial chair with a revolving door. McNeill had the hot potato taken away from him; it passed quickly from Liam Brady (inexperienced) to Lou Macari (over-hardened) to Tommy Burns, who ascended the throne only after the old order had collapsed.

MICK MAHER   When my father died in 1990 I came back from New Zealand; and Billy McNeill's mother came round to the house before the funeral to pay her respects and whatnot. And she said – what is it they say in Glasgow – 'his jacket's on a shoogly peg'. Months before it happened his family knew he wasn't going to last.

GERRY MULVENNA   I thought that it wasn't right that Liam Brady should have been allowed to serve a managerial apprenticeship with Celtic; the job was too big for him. The guy just seemed to be lost at times; he was at sea; and he may turn out to be one of the greatest managers that the world has ever seen, but he shouldn' t have been cutting his teeth on Celtic.

191

TONY GRIFFIN Macari was obviously the old board's man. I was never fond of Macari as a player; he took – or seemed to take – the first opportunity to be off. The story, probably apocryphal, always went that he had gambling debts and that his slice of the transfer deal went to paying off his debts; whether that's true or not I don't know. The important thing is that he didn't show any great loyalty to Celtic then, and I didn't feel much better about him when he came back as manager.

DAVIE HAY I think that the last five years – 1990 until 1995 – have been the most traumatic in the club's history. Prior to that there had only been four or five managers. Before me we had Maley, McStay, McGrory, Stein, McNeill; since then myself, McNeill again, Brady, Macari, Burns; the same number in that period of time. Traumatic.

Distraction number 2: the importation by these managers – and the consequent barracking by the supporters – of a number of players whom the fans felt were substandard or supernumerary.

  Get rid of that lump of lard! . . .

STEVEN GALL The thing Celtic had sadly been missing for a long time was a big, out-and-out striker – somebody big and powerful about the penalty box who could use his head. And when we signed Cascarino for a million pounds everybody's going, 'Here's a guy who's going to do a job . . .' We waited about fourteen games. At last the guy scores against Rangers and all is forgiven. For about a week. Then it was back to 'Get rid of that lump of lard!'

TOMMY HYNDMAN I was brought up with great players. But in recent years we've signed some real donkeys – people who shamed the hoops. Tony Cannyscoreagoalo, Wayne Biggins – there've been plenty.

SANDY STRANG When Celtic re-signed Bonner they had a plethora of goalkeepers. Bonner, Muggleton, Marshall, Kerr as well . . . I can't remember them all. There was a one-liner going about that Celtic now had six goalies on their books, one for every day of the week except Saturday.

Distraction number 3: the board's response to the grim state of Celtic Park and the increasingly gleaming Ibrox – apparently rock-solid plans to move Celtic to a superstadium in Cambuslang. The plan proved to be – in more ways than one – without a solid foundation.

TOMMY HYNDMAN What really annoyed us was that Rangers announced that they were going to add a bit to the Broomloan Stand or whatever, and that they were going to spend five million pounds on one bit of the stadium. And the *Evening Times* said, 'What have you done, Mr Kelly?' The answer was that we'd painted the steps yellow; or done some work on the pie-stalls or something.

GERRY DEVLIN It was at a Hearts game – we were in the stand – a couple of seasons ago. There were some Hearts supporters there. One went off, and when he came back he said, 'I wish you would just put some shite down on the floor of that toilet and take the bad look aff the place.'

FRANK GLENCROSS There was all this talk about moving to Cambuslang; all airy-fairy talk.

JIMMY FINNIS Superstadia and all these big numbers were floating about – so many hundred million pounds and Celtic were going to a new purpose-built at Cambuslang . . . it was disappointing, a shambles.

STEVEN GALL The biggest joke about Cambuslang for me was that they hired all sorts of guys like Superstadia, guys like Patrick Nally or Patrick Lally or whatever he was called, and they'd these guys out doing surveys or something. And I think the ground was full of plutonium or some kind of dangerous chemicals and it was sinking; it was built on a pit-shaft, maybe – so they were asking kids to go out and look for holes in the ground, advertised in a full-page spread in the *Evening Times*! So you'd umpteen irate mothers on the phone to Celtic saying their weans' legs were broken out looking for holes for them . . .

. . . the board bled the club dry . . .

TOMMY HYNDMAN   The board bled the club dry. The Cambuslang thing was the final straw. A lot of people who weren't interested in the politics of the club – who just wanted to see a team on the park winning things – turned against the board then. We'd done the nine-in-a-row, the European Cup, the name of Celtic was known all over the world, yet you'd guys on the board who couldn't run a household. Those guys who'd no interest in politics of Celtic just said, 'We've had enough – they've got to go.' And that's when things started happening – the boycott and things like that.

Distraction number 4: ridding the boardroom of the families – the Kellys, the Whites and the Grants – who, in the eyes of the fans, had run Celtic so badly for so long.

STEVEN GALL   You started getting a string of bad results. It'd been getting progressively worse for years. But that season, 1993–94, had been our best to date, and come the turn of the year we were still in the hunt for everything. Had we beaten Rangers in the Ne'erday match, we'd actually have leap-frogged them. What happened is that they beat us 4–2; and it wasn't so much the result as the manner of it. Most people were still trying to get in the ground and it was 2–0 to Rangers. And that game is what really gave the anti-board feeling a full head of steam.

TOMMY HYNDMAN   Pretty soon after that – well, the players must have got sick, because every time the players scored a goal there wasn't a chant of a certain player's name or a 'Hail! Hail! The Celts are here . . .' There was just 'Sack the Board!' 'Sack the Board!' and it was constant.

   Now I don't know about yourself, but if anybody was wanting me out of a job that much, I'd resign, I'd quit. The board didn't go. Finally it all came to a head at a game against

Kilmarnock at Parkhead. That was the day the fox appeared. It was a night match and this fox came out of the darkness and ran the full length of the park and the crowd started singing, 'There's only two Michael Kellys.'

The other thing that happened at that match was that the T-shirts turned up. Now you could take any banner in you wanted, so long as it didn't say 'Sack the Board' on it. So the inventiveness of certain individuals came up with T-shirts and sweatshirts with individual letters on them, when you put them together, they all stood together at the Rangers end, and it said, SACK THE BOARD. There was something detrimental about Michael Kelly – about Doctor Devious, as they called him – on the back.

FRANK GLENCROSS   I didn't like that conduct. I think it was unCeltic-like. It gave other supporters something to laugh about. I didn't like those scenes, the chanting, this body must go or that body must go. You have to make a protest some way, otherwise the board might think they're doing okay. But I think the best way to protest is – if you don't like what's going on then just stay away.

You're no Celtic supporter behaving like that . . .

EDDIE McGRAW   What happened was terrible. All along the line I never liked the way they went about displacing the directors. At the end of the day the directors needed displaced. But at that time I didn't like all this 'Kelly, get to f***' and all that kind of stuff. I never joined in. I fell out with a couple of guys who said to me, 'Are you no singing, auld yin?' 'Naw,' I said, 'and I'm no going to talk to you either – you're no Celtic supporter behaving like that.'

JIM MacDONALD   I was really wanting to go to the Kilmarnock game – everybody wanted to go. But we all ended up sat in the pub. I was getting the fanzines, *Not the View* and *Once a Tim*, and they were urging you not to. So we ended up not going. We ended up sitting in Baird's Bar in the Gallowgate – a real Celtic house – on the night of the game. There were millions of Celtic fans there – it was packed out. It was as if it was an hour before the match. They had the radio on and we were all singing. The fans who'd left at half-time or with 20 minutes to go came in after a while – there was no fighting or anything, but people were still saying, 'I don't think you should have gone.' They were saying, 'We came out at half-time like we said we were going to.' And we were going, 'But you've still given them the money.' I didn't see any of the ones who stayed the whole 90 minutes – they seemed to have just gone home straight away.

TOMMY HYNDMAN   It meant you had fan against fan, very much civil war material. One group had asked that you leave after the hour mark; one group had asked that you don't go at all, to join the boycott. You'd people standing outside with counters – somebody hired private census-takers to count people in, and they were going to be standing outside. When people started moving outside you started to get a wee bit of animosity. There was a lot of strife. But it wasn't long afterwards Brian Dempsey made the announcement – 'The battle's over, the rebels have won.'

STEVEN GALL   There was a lot of bad blood and there still is bad blood; you still hear it on the terracings, in the seats at Hampden, supporters bickering at one another. It divided a lot of people, a lot of families. It's time for Celtic fans to be united – we can see that wee bit of light at the end of the tunnel. You've got a whole new management structure, a whole new board, when you see the plans for the ground it's going to be super to be sitting in . . .

GEORGE MOORE   Of course the Celtic support will recover. Celtic supporters will always come back. These two guys will probably not remember, but in the early '60s, when Rangers were dominant, winning Trebles and Leagues and different things, it was Michael Kelly's relative, Sir Bob Kelly, that was in charge. I stood there and barracked the man, 'Get out Kelly, Kelly must go,' until he brought Jock Stein. Kelly was Mr Wonderful after that.

BRIAN McBRIDE   It happens with football clubs, it happens with companies. It's only when a club's doing badly that you look at how it's run, you look at the finances, you look at the people in charge. A successful club would never have had that dirty washing on the front pages. I think it's quite sad what's happened – but I'm sure it's part of a cycle. If you look at Rangers now, they're probably on the decline, though they've had five or six great years. Whereas fifteen or twenty years ago Celtic were at their peak, and Rangers were nowhere.

Even with a new manager in place in the shape of Tommy Burns and a new board led by Fergus McCann, Celtic have had to endure indignities. The perfect start the Burns regime would have craved was denied them in the League Cup final against First Division Raith Rovers.

TOMMY HYNDMAN   On that disastrous doom-filled day at Ibrox Park . . . We were all pretty nervous – going in against a team like Raith Rovers. At the time Celtic weren't scoring many goals and Raith Rovers were scoring a barrowload – so you're thinking to yourself, there's going to be a game here anyway. When Charlie popped up and scored to make it 2–1 you're thinking, yes, that's it – but for a goalkeeper to lose concentration with four minutes to go – suicidal. So then you're going through to the non-event, the extra-time; then the penalty shoot-out. When Paul McStay finally went up and placed the ball I said to myself, he's missing this. The unspeakable happened. Goodnight Vienna. I went back to the club that evening, trying to be a bit philosophical about things, it's not the end of the world . . . but there were people who couldn't believe it, people greeting in their beer.

> . . . *on the bus on which I travel not one of the men went to work the next day. Not one . . .*

MARGARET DEVLIN   I didn't see any of the penalties; I had my back turned; I just kept saying, 'Please, God, just this once.' I could have cried. Not for me, because Celtic lost; not for Celtic;

but for Paul McStay. On the bus on which I travel none of the men went to work the next day. Not one. They just could not face it.

Celtic's long wait for a sliver of light at the end of their tunnel came when they recaptured the Scottish Cup on May 27th, 1995.

GERRY MULVENNA They played very poorly, in point of fact; got the early goal and hung on to it. They had to win and were probably nervous, probably worried; Airdrie came into it in the second half. It was a fairly even game, if truth be told. But the result was all that mattered.

ADAM SHIELS I couldn't get in, couldn't get a ticket anywhere, even from quite reliable sources. I stood down there at the ground until about about twenty past two, then got in the car and dived back to Hamilton to watch it on telly; I had my programme and my papers and that kind of thing, of course. I did see myself on Sky – everybody was saying to me, 'Saw you at the game . . .' But I wasn't. Anyway, we won it. What a relief was that! Don't get me wrong, it was a terrible game and a terrible performance. But nothing mattered except winning; I'm still trying to savour it.

TONY GRIFFIN The game was dreadful, a shocker, an embarrassingly bad game. I watched it with a friend from England, a Chelsea supporter, and I was just cringing. At the end I didn't feel any great elation; just relief perhaps, a feeling or a hope that this might be the precursor to better days in the future.

TOMMY HYNDMAN The future? Five years on? We'll have five Leagues in a row, five European Cups in a row. We'll not have any Grants or Kellys or Whites on the board, but guys with a bit of knowledge. We'll have gone back to a refurbished Celtic Park and everybody's going to be scared to come to Celtic Park again. Sixty-thousand, one of the best stadiums in Britain, seeing

Tommy Burns coming out to defend his League Championship for the third time. Dream on . . .

Meanwhile, in Europe . . .
Only when Walter Smith took over and the Champions' League, in its nascent form, had arrived did Rangers put together a decent run. They never really looked like they would go all the way, but victories over Leeds and an exciting double header with Marseille were counter-evidence against the accusation that they were just a big fish in a small pond.

. . . guys don't show emotion like that, unless it's drink and football comes together . . .

COLIN LAMOND The most vivid memory I have of any game is of not being at the game. It was the second game of the Leeds–Rangers European Cup tie. All the Rangers fans were banned from Elland Road, so about twelve of us from the Linwood Supporters Club went down to the Edmiston Club and watched the game on the big screen, on television. There were about a thousand Rangers supporters there, a big carnival atmosphere. My brother had come back from Saudi for it. When we won, there were literally men kissing men, kissing each other, it was like the end of the world, people were almost in tears – because that's when it really hit home that the people in England would have to sit up and take notice of Rangers and what we stood for. I remember hundreds of pint glasses ending up on the floor, because people were falling on the tables – the place was a mess. I remember hugging my brother and actually rolling on the floor in front of the giant screen. Amazing – you don't really get that – guys don't show emotion like that, unless it's drink and football comes together.

SUSAN AMBROSE Getting into the league section was just phenomenal – it was a great atmosphere. European nights are great nights – I hope they come back. All the flags, the banners – there was one that just about covered the whole of the Copland Road top deck, it was astonishing. The singing, the chanting . . .

COLIN LAMOND   Once we got to the round robin part of the competition – well, there was great intensity in the crowd on these evenings. There's obviously virtually no opposition fans in these European games – it's our own atmosphere we're generating, it's not against anyone, it's just together – it was more intense than an Old Firm game.

The Marseille one – we had a feeling, oh no, not again. They went 2–0 up and basically – well, we were 2–0 down and it looked like we could have lost 5–0. Abidi Pele stood out that day, we couldn't get the ball off him, and certain players were looking pretty bad, looking quite ordinary. But the comeback was to epitomise and to stand for the rest of the European season.

ALAN GALLOWAY The last ten minutes against Marseille were something special. It says on one of the videos I've seen that we had four foreigners playing for us that night – Mikhailichenko, Hateley, Steven and Houdini.

COLIN LAMOND   Coming back from adversity – in the next game, against Bruges, Hateley got sent off but Nisbet scored a goal, a real fluke, it hit a bit of mud and almost, like a frisbee almost.

> . . . *everybody just stood up because the ball had just the most peculiar arc on it . . .*

SUSAN AMBROSE   Rangers had been putting Bruges under a hell of a lot of pressure and all sorts of shots and crosses had been raining in, but nothing was happening. Nissy was just so frustrated when he picked up this ball that he just skelped it and it took a deflection. Everybody just stood up because this ball had just the most peculiar arc on it – and all of a sudden it bounced in front of the goalkeeper and right over him. It was just the most incredible release of joy that we'd scored – but there was also laughter because it was the most bizarre goal ever seen. An amazing moment.

DOUGIE DICK Marseille at Marseilles – I made a bit of a fool of myself saying that we were going to the European Cup final – but that was one of the highlights. We had a great crack on the bus trip going down. We left Dover at eight o'clock; a fantastic time at Avignon, with three buses stopped there. Into the game – great crack with the Marseille fans. What got us was that the Marseille fans, who were used to intimidating away fans, were intimidated by us – because I don't think they'd seen so many drunks in their life, just stoating about, falling about all over the place – that was great. The game was fantastic – the whole thing about being only 90 minutes away from the European Cup final.

COLIN LAMOND It all came to an end against CSKA Moscow, though I think we knew it had all ended when we didn't beat Marseille over in France. I took my radio to Ibrox. Radio Clyde were covering the Marseille–Bruges game, and I sort of knew that even if we won 2–0 or 3–0 against CSKA Moscow we weren't going through anyway. But there was only a point in it at the end.

RICHARD GOUGH We had the breaks right from the start, we had the run of the ball. Against Lyngby in the first game they were through twice in the first ten minutes and hit the post each time. Two-nil down against Marseille and we came back. Nisbet's goal. That year we went unbeaten for about 30 games; we just seemed to be on a roll; sometimes it is uncanny.

DOUGIE DICK That last game against CSKA Moscow – I tell you, it was tears and everything. But it was just brilliant, because, with five minutes to go – remember, a criticism of a lot of Rangers fans is that they leave too early – the whole crowd all just got up and started singing 'We'll Support You Evermore.' It wasn't because of that night – we knew we hadn't got there – we understood that we were out. That was just a thank you for the whole season.

Celtic had to look on and watch all this; few European games stick out from their decade of further European decline.

MICK McCARTHY We had a couple of trips in Europe but not much success. We went to Honved and lost 1–0 and then took four off them back at Parkhead. That was a great night; it gave you a sense of what they all said about European nights at Celtic, made you feel disappointed that we didn't see more of them. Night matches are exciting anyway, but night matches in Europe with the eyes of the world upon you, and with whole success that Celtic had had years before made it special. They were big matches. But we went on and lost to Dortmund or Bremen; I can't remember.

TOMMY HYNDMAN One of the worst European nights was against Partizan Belgrade. Jackie Dziekanowski, who I'll never forget, scores four goals and still ends up on the losing team!

STEVEN GALL The game kicked off and Celtic went a goal down right away, which really meant they had to constantly chase the game – they'd lost 2–1 away. They went up, equalised. Lost another stupid goal, 2–1 down, chasing again. They got it back. It's 3–2 to them, three each, Celtic forge ahead, 4–3, then they go 5–3 up. So we're clear, only a minute to go, we were there – and I says to my pal, 'C'mon we'll start singing – it's over and easy.' And he says, 'Aye.' And see as soon as he turned round to start singing, that was it, they scored, the whole place went flat. Up to 5–3 it'd been quite surreal; at 5–3 it was total bedlam, then the place did erupt. What I thought was their downfall that night – Celtic made a substitution – and European teams are kind of noted for taking the furthest man on the park off and making him trudge, slowly, feigning injury by the means of limping or holding a bandaged head – but Celtic took off the guy that was standing near to their own dug-out – he's straight off instead of the guy in the corner walking off nice and slow. Only a minute to go. Next thing Partizan have broken up the field. It was such a strange feeling coming out after that game – did it really happen?

TOMMY HYNDMAN There was an emptiness about everybody coming out. To be so elated one minute, then to be in the depths of despair the next . . . Football.

It may be bad not having teams who can do well in Europe –
but it could be quite a lot worse.

JOE SHEVLIN   In 1989 myself and Jim Williamson, as Celtic
club stewards, were asked if we'd like a trip to Yugoslavia to
assist with the game against Partizan Belgrade. We joined the
team on Sunday morning and arrived in Dubrovnik in the early
evening. After dinner we explored the city. On the Monday the
team flew to Mostar. Jim and I walked around the walls, harbour
and churches. On the Tuesday we left for the game by coach and
visited Medjugorje; we were in time for mass, but no one was
allowed to enter the church wearing shorts; it was amusing to
see the fans giving their mates a loan of their trousers to enter
the church. Then the game. Celtic were up against a tough team
and the playing surface was awful; losing 2–1 didn't seem such a
bad result. We arrived back in Glasgow on the next evening. I
regret not going back the following year. Now the walls I walked
around have been shelled; the Belvedere Hotel has been
bombed; Mostar has been destroyed. I saw pictures on TV of
the football pitch where we had been, with dead bodies and pris-
oners. I could only think of Bill Shankly, about football being a
matter of more than life and death.

Chapter Eleven

RIVALRY

In the first chapter of this book, supporters and players testified to their devotion to their clubs; for all the differences between club and club, between supporter and supporter, that level of devotion amongst their followers remains something the clubs share. Another thing they share is a participation in a tradition of rivalry which at one level ('the greatest derby in the world', etc., etc., etc.) is a healthy sporting contest, but which is, on another, an excuse for quasi-religious bigotry which has for too long brought violence to, and shame on, the people of Glasgow.

There remains some question about the true nature of this rivalry; sectarianism, if you prefer. On the one hand you have the outpouring, torrential hatred visible and audible on the terraces on the day of an Old Firm match; the noise and intensity of this vocalisation of hatred never fails to shock. On the other hand, Glasgow is no Beirut; its citizens walk down shared streets. In almost all areas of everyday life Rangers and Celtic supporters merge happily, talk happily, slag each other off happily, in spite of songs sung on terraces that are deeply hateful to each other.

Clearly there is a deal of two-facedness in behaviour. Clearly there are bigots amongst the support. But equally clearly, a lot of the bigotry – Celtic's mindless pro-IRA chanting, the equally mindless loyalist songs of the opposition – is ritual rather than felt. Look a little deeper beneath and you do find a pride, a confrontational pride even, in the way fans of both sides cling to their own cultural identities; but you also find a population the bulk of which simply gets on with it, carries on its normal business in the manner of normal rivals.

NEIL McDERMOTT   I detest the Old Firm matches; because the atmosphere is nothing short of poisonous. It's sheer hatred. The only thing that can be said in its favour is that the 'yahoo' element vent their spleen on each other at a distance, whereas the same people could be in Belfast shooting each other or whatever, killing each other. So at least there's that release for their pent-up emotions.

BRIAN McBRIDE   I think without a doubt an Old Firm match is one of the most exciting, thrilling and I think frightening spectacles you could ever be involved in. I've taken friends from England, friends from abroad to some of these matches. They've read about them but they've never quite believed that they're everything they're made out to be. And afterwards, I've had Newcastle fans or Liverpool fans, who thought they had big derbies, coming out of there with their knees shaking.

COLIN GLASS   I've not missed one at Ibrox or Hampden since I started watching Rangers. But if you asked me if I liked them or not, I'd have to say I still don't know. Because the feeling you get in your stomach . . .

GEORGE SHERIDAN   Old Firm games were too tense – they were never games you could enjoy unless you were winning easily, and even then you had to go through the period before you got on top. With a lot of guys, that was the one game they particularly wanted to see. I'm afraid with me I wasn't particularly bothered.

HUGH FERRIE   I tended to avoid the Rangers games. I didn't like all the abuse they were hurling at one another. There was no objectivity about the game – people couldn't stand back and appreciate good football. If you were a Rangers fan you couldn't see anything good in Celtic's play and vice versa.

SANDY STRANG   The people who were around you at these matches were utterly blinkered. Often very boring, too, if you got one chap who wanted to vent his wrath. And the referee was always biased. By definition, the referee was failing to spot the nuances of the game. When he gave a decision that was in your favour he was always right. It was never the obverse of that partisan coin – there was never an admission that we were lucky to get that penalty for example – in that case the referee was just doing the job he should be doing.

TOMMY HYNDMAN   Before an Old Firm game kicks off it's sheer hatred. For 90 minutes it's sheer hatred. After the game it's sheer hatred. A lot of people would have you believe that that's the way it is all the time, but it's not true. A lot of Celtic and a lot of Rangers fans are really, really friendly with each other; there's a lot of banter goes on. But then you get the bigots who can't see past the end of their noses. But, basically, if there wasn't a Rangers there wouldn't be a strong Celtic; if there wasn't a Celtic there wouldn't be a strong Rangers. You need one to have the other. Most fans realise that.

BRIAN CRAIG   If you're talking about Old Firm games, then even if you scrape it 1–0 with a last minute penalty you're still on a high. You get up early for work. If it's 1–0 to them you don't want to go to work. If I go into work I don't gloat about it to the Celtic supporters who I know go to the games; because I know they're in the same boat as I've been in; and when they're at work they don't gloat about it for the same reason. I think that everybody who knows what I'm talking about and supports the Old Firm knows it's the people who don't go who are the ones who are most vocal at the work; and who don't appreciate what it means to get beat.

For the players the equation is a little less emotionally complicated, though they too are drawn into the well of hatred and tension.

MATT LYNCH   There was always a lot of argy-bargy in the Old Firm game; there is no question about it. One of the reasons for that was that you were put on a special bonus for that game. Before the war the bonus was normally £2; when you played the

Rangers it was £10. So it wasn't just the colour of the blue jersey that got you going; there was a number of players in our team that in their young days would have wanted to wear that jersey. But when the bonus was on offer, they forgot about that and got stuck in with the rest of us. It was important to cash in.

TOMMY GEMMELL   In Celtic–Rangers matches I would probably be playing against, say, Willie Henderson, and wee Willie was kind of half-blind; he wore contact lenses and I mean wee Willie would be the first to tell you, I never at any time hurt him, but we had the odd body-check and the odd trip and so forth. And the Rangers supporters would be screaming blue murder for my blood and I would be picking wee Willie up and saying, 'I'll see you in Reid's Bar after the match.' That is what we normally did. There were about three or four Celtic players and three or four Rangers players who met in this bar in Hope Street in Glasgow and had a few beers after the game.

DAVID McKINNON   It's the only game I've played in where when you walk out the hairs on the back of your neck stand up; the Rangers supporters are all so committed, the Celtic supporters too. I remember standing in the tunnel with Murdo MacLeod, my cousin, before the 4–4 game; and I remember patting him on the backside and saying, 'Well, all the best, partner.' And we go onto the pitch and in the first minute he goes over the ball and into me! I said, 'I'm going to kill you' – it was that kind of atmosphere when you were playing.

COLIN GLASS   One thing I've always found fascinating about Old Firm games was that the police used to print notices in the paper about routes that fans should follow to the games. It was a complete waste of money. Fans always followed their traditional routes to the game without any police instruction and I can still leave my house in Bearsden to go to an Old Firm game at Ibrox and not see a single Celtic fan until I'm inside that park, just because of the routes I take and the routes they will take. It seems to be traditional segregation without any need for statutory control.

NEIL McDERMOTT   Where I stayed in Dennistoun I could go to Celtic Park, Celtic–Rangers matches, which I did for years, and never pass a Rangers supporter, because of the segregation at the games. When I walked along Duke Street and went down to the Gallowgate area, it was the Celtic End of the ground that you would arrive at. You quite literally would not pass a Rangers supporter. London Road was a different matter. That was where the Rangers fans would come, up from the Brigton Cross area.

The roots of the great divide that separates Celtic and Rangers are not difficult to trace. Though not quite a holy war, the feelings of antagonism are at least partly religious in origin. The waters are muddy, though; parts of the traditions of the clubs are indigenous, parts are foreign bodies.

SANDY STRANG A nice one-liner I heard a few years ago was the Glaswegian definition of an atheist: a bloke who goes to a Rangers–Celtic match to watch the football.

CHARLIE LOGAN In Scotland, with segregated schools, you're almost bound to be a Rangers fan if you go to a Protestant school. A non-denominational school, sorry. You're bound to be a Celtic supporter if you go to a Catholic school – that follows as night follows day.

IAIN PATTERSON Rangers is the more natural focus of support for someone from a state school; obviously if you were in a Catholic school you would tend to support Celtic. In recent polls – one was in *Scotland on Sunday* – it seemed that Asians in Glasgow tend to support Rangers rather than Celtic – the reason I would suggest is that they tend to go to state schools and therefore their friends will support Rangers and therefore they will support Rangers. I think there is a similar situation in Edinburgh – Asians tend to support Hearts rather than Hibs.

JAMES DUNBAR I think it still matters that Celtic represents the West of Scotland Catholic community – I still believe that that is a big drawing point for Celtic. Any young kid that goes to a Catholic school in the West of Scotland supports Celtic. It goes beyond that, though; for myself Celtic is the one great stable thing in life – things may change but Celtic is always there. You're sitting there in the stand and the priests are there and all the rest of it – it's a very stable entity.

ALAN GALLOWAY   It's tribalism, isn't it – it's belonging to the mass that is Rangers. I suppose that a lot of being a Rangers fan is what's bred into you, and what you've learned is what's acceptable and what you are – you follow the team, it's in your system, you feel as though you belong to it; it's machoism, it's tribalism I suppose; you feel that at a young age. That sort of forms you to a team and if you get that you've got that in your blood forever.

CHARLIE GALLAGHER   I came from the Gorbals and every Saturday half of the Gorbals would be at Celtic Park; a lot of people respected me because I played there. With my people being Irish, when I went over to Ireland I was Charlie Gallagher of Celtic – that's who I was. I felt the same way when I was capped for Ireland. I'm Irish at heart though I was born and brought up in Scotland.

EUGENE MacBRIDE   You were Irish. I got soul from old 78 rpm records and it was all 'Soldiers of The Legion of the Rearguard' and 'The Boys from the County Wexford' – all these Irish songs that my father and my mother had accumulated, all these records, and I used to put them on the old wind-up gramophone. When soul came out in the 1960s I understood what soul meant. It wasn't James Brown for me – it was Ireland.

MICK MAHER   I know everybody would probably say this about their own teams but I do think that Celtic are a wee bit different – probably because of their background and so on. I remember going to see *The Celtic Story* and bumping into a guy I hadn't seen since I left school and I got talking to him again and he said, 'Do you know what this story's about? It's about us.' I said, 'What do you mean?' He said, 'Well what was your grandfather?' I said, 'My grandfather came from Kildare, he worked for the railways.' 'Yes, and mine came from Donegal and was a labourer – and look at us now, two generations later. I'm a psychiatrist and you're in insurance' – the inference was that Celtic had grown at the same time as our community had grown.

JOHN WATSON The Northern Ireland thing is certainly a big thing because Scotland and Northern Ireland have always been very close. Since people from the chapel founded Celtic and they wear the Celtic Cross in their badge, naturally Northern Irish that came over to Scotland signed up on the Rangers side. And Rangers never signed Catholics – the bottom line was that that was where the big connection with Northern Ireland came. The Orange Order always went to Ibrox for their annual parade.

IAIN PATTERSON The song I think that epitomises Rangers and their support is 'We Are The People'. The concept behind it is essentially Calvinistic – We Are The Elect. If you look at the names of some Rangers supporters' clubs you'll see names like the Bellshill Chosen Few – 'Chosen Few' is a name, like Loyal, that they tend to put after their name.

How much has the Irish question shaped the rivalry of Rangers and Celtic? Evidence for it is that there are lots of Union flags, lots of Irish tricolours, and the songs are Ulster loyalist/Irish republican and obviously some have come across the North channel.

But I don't think the Rangers–Celtic rivalry could exist with that alone as the input, and I don't think sectarian friction in Scotland is the result of a foreign bacillus or whatever you'd call it. You've got to look at segregated schools – I don't think sectarianism would have lasted so long if it had just been the result of a few people coming across the sea and joining in; that would have been a tail wagging the dog. If you look at the Liverpool–Everton rivalry you can see Red Hands of Ulster and Irish tricolours there – but to the Liverpool public these are things that are attached on – it doesn't make it a sectarian fixture. Most of the causes must be local.

SANDY STRANG My grandfather was a very meek, quiet man, a watchmaker who brought up a large family in

Pollokshaws. To see the man he became at the football; this man was transported into a rampant bigot. It wasn't so much the hatred of the opposition as a total identification with the people on his own side. One time Henderson was running down the wing – it was one of these A-team games – and some left-back or other kept arriving with late tackles. I remember I was sitting beside my uncle and my grandfather and Henderson took off down the wing and this left-back came in from behind – it was quite clear that Henderson couldn't see it – and my grandfather stood up and shouted, 'Watch it, Wullie! Mind your legs, son!' And I remember my uncle turned to me and said, 'You know, he was never as solicitous as that about his own flesh and blood.'

The ramifications of religious bigotry – of us and them – weren't a significant factor. Occasionally there were references round the table to 'it was great beating them'. You existed because you competed and you had to have someone to compete against to make it a competition, and it would all have been invalidated if you didn't have this great opposite. Obviously social background, quasi-religious background and different ways of going about one's life was part of the package of the opposites.

FRANK GLENCROSS I belong to the Dumfries Celtic Supporters Club. In this area, the sectarian issue doesn't apply – in the Dalbeattie Celtic Supporters Club there are hardly any Catholics! Nobody thinks of religion like they do in the city. You're bound by your religious beliefs up there – whatever particular school you went to, what church you go to. Up there it's treason to do anything like this but down here I've known joint buses go up to a Celtic–Rangers game.

Until recently, Rangers carried one important black mark. Just as South Africa distinguished itself from a thousand other repressive regimes by institutionalising racism, so Rangers institutionalised their sectarianism with their fixed policy of not signing Catholic players. For Celtic fans this was proof positive that the kettle was black. For Rangers' fans the distinction between a club that institutionalised sectarianism and one that merely had the trappings of it was an over-fine one.

JOHN LAWSON   I played football myself. I remember in the old Glasgow Empire being with an uncle of one of my pals who played for Rangers during the war and being introduced to the chief scout of Rangers, when I was 16 years old. The conversation went, 'Do you play football, John?' And the immediate reply from my pal – 'Aye, but you canny sign him – he goes to the Chapel in the morning.'

HUGH FERRIE   The great thing about Celtic was that they never asked a player what his religion was. There were players like Bobby Hogg – the Celtic captain in the late '30s – who wasn't a Catholic. Ronnie Simpson. Stein himself. Rangers were different – if they wanted to sign someone and saw a holy picture in the house then they walked out.

DANNY McGRAIN   There is the old story going about that Rangers didn't sign me because of my name – Daniel Fergus McGrain – it sounds Irish. All I know is that I was playing for Queen's Park and the school at 16; a friend of my dad's was at a game with a Rangers scout and was trying to punt me as a player, and the scout said, 'We've looked at him but he's a Catholic.' My dad's friend said, 'No he's not; he goes to Kingsridge Secondary in Drumchapel – a Protestant school.' The scout said, 'Yeah, okay,' as if he'd looked into all the details already and as if he didn't want to be looked on as if he hadn't done the job properly. In the end I played for Scottish Schools against England at Hampden; we were hammered 4–1, and I mean hammered; these English guys, their under-18s, were all giants and we were just typical wee Scottish schoolboys – I think they were all smoking, drinking – undernourished! I got carried off with cramp but Sean Fallon signed me on an S-form for Celtic; and that was it.

CHARLIE GALLAGHER   The majority of the boys playing in the '60s did support Celtic before they went there – we were supporters as well as players. Willie Wallace was a Rangers supporter, so they say. One day we were at Tynecastle when he was still with Hearts and he called me a papist b! When he ended up at Celtic Park I said, 'Do you remember what you said?' He said, 'What difference does it make now?'.

CHARLIE LOGAN The great myth of Scottish football is that Jock Stein walked on water. He did well for Celtic. But one thing I heard about Jock Stein is that if he was watching two players and one was Catholic and one was Protestant and they were equal, then he would take the Protestant; he would sign the Protestant because Rangers wouldn't sign a Catholic. And that very statement is bigotry in its own way – bigotry against the Catholic player. Now maybe he knew that he would get the Catholic too, because Rangers wouldn't take him – but it's bigotry none the less.

BILL McARTHUR My objections to Celtic? They flew a foreign flag above the stand; their directors held foreign passports; their profits went to a foreign country; yet they took their money from Glasgow, from Glaswegians.

JIM COOKE I've always maintained that whereas Rangers were always criticised for being bigots, Celtic were more bigoted than Rangers were. Okay, I admit Celtic played Protestants in their team, but their attitude outwith the team was more bigoted than Rangers'.

JOHN WATSON The Rangers Protestant traditions are still there. But Rangers has changed. You can't hold yourself back. If you want to stick to one creed, you've got limitations. The people who are running Rangers now are very broad-minded – they're working for the best. You're not going to get that if you're only going to play Protestants from Glasgow. You've got to go all over Europe. Maurice Johnston was the big one at the time – but even now I'd rather he was lining up on our side than lining up against us.

Experiences of fans and players suggest that, notwithstanding the cultural divide within the city, we should perhaps take some elements of the Old Firm rivalry with – if not a spoonful of sugar – then at least a pinch of salt.

DOUG BAILLIE   I came from a mining village to the south of Lanark, where I didn't know a Catholic from a Protestant or a Protestant from a Catholic. I played for Airdrie for four years before joining Rangers and the Rangers–Celtic thing was a culture shock. When I played for Airdrie against Rangers I was all the Catholic so-and-sos of the day; when I played for Airdrie against Celtic I was all the Protestant so-and-sos of the day. So when I signed for Rangers the Celtic supporters were proved right all along.

I have a son who played and signed for Celtic as luck would have it; the Rangers weren't interested. I have Rangers supporters to this day who won't speak to me because my son signed for Celtic. That's a small-minded thing; nothing you can do about it.

JIM COOKE   You still hear people shouting Fenian this and that; and you get them saying, you orange bs. I never wear colours; I've got scarves and ties but I never wear colours when I go to football; but for some reason some people around here seem to know you're a Rangers supporter; waiting out there for a bus you get called an orange b, which I'm not. Yes, you still get orange b's and Fenian b's and all the rest of that.

DENIS CONNAGHAN   When you went to Somerset Park or Motherwell the crowds were pretty close and you heard everything they wanted to call you; sometimes you could catch some of the things they threw at you as well. It happens even in junior football; you know, somebody for whatever reason remembers a bad goal or a great save or you injuring one of their players and what that person seems to be there for is to remind you of what you've done the last time you were there. I remember one time playing junior football for Arthurlie and we were playing Baillieston. I made one of my few great saves late on in the game; we were wining 1–0 and I touched the ball over the bar. And this female called me a dirty Fenian bastard. I thought, 'This is junior football – I've been away from Celtic four years.' I turned and said, 'Do you mind telling me what my religion or

215

anything else has got to do with junior football between Baillieston and Arthurlie?' She just shut up right away.

JOHN LARKIN The Celtic fans called Billy Bremner an orange bastard when he played against them at Hampden; when he equalised it was 'ya dirty orange bastard!' And he's a Catholic, a Celtic fan. It's a funny side of Celtic fans – it doesn't matter who's playing against them, they're orange.

IAIN PATTERSON People sort of use the term 'Fenian bastard' as just an extension of the word bastard – I don't like this person. Or we're against this person. Plenty of Protestants – and plenty of ex-Rangers players – have been called Fenian bastards when they've returned to Ibrox. One of the most rabidly loyalist players – known to be a loyalist – was Michael O'Neil of Motherwell. It was reported in the paper that one of the Rangers players had called him a Fenian bastard. He scored against Celtic in the Cup semi-final the year Motherwell won it.

I can remember at the 1–0 game, the League Cup semi-final a couple of years back – Rangers won it 1–0, thanks to Hateley – that Alan Main and John Clark of Dundee United were in the Rangers part of the stand; they were actually holding a Union Jack that had been passed to them by Rangers fans in the enclosure. But the next time Rangers played Dundee United Alan Main was called a Fenian bastard by some fans, so . . .

SCOT DICKSON I'm in a bit of a confused position, being a Catholic and a Rangers supporter. I've always tried to ignore the religious bigotry which surrounds Rangers and Celtic. I came to support Rangers because my father was a Rangers supporter and I was taken to matches from a very young age. I wish the bigotry could be stamped out altogether. You still get the chants – both Rangers and Celtic songs are songs of bigotry, I suppose, if you analyse them; and I do sing them myself, even though I'm against all this.

ANDY ROBERTSON I would say it's a minority who actually mean what they say when they're singing. Everybody can call everybody all your Fenian b's and your orange b's. But I would say that the only time they really get on at each other is when they've got a drink in them or something like that. In those cases the religion is just an excuse for fighting. I know Celtic fans in Larkhall and I get on great with them – I respect them and they respect me.

DOUGIE DICK   When Celtic were making an offer for the bulbs from the Hampden floodlights this mate of mine rang up Celtic and said, 'I've just been clearing out my loft and I've found some fairy lights. Would you like to make me an offer?' The paupers . . . the unwashed – it's easy to ridicule them.

TOMMY HYNDMAN   My wife's a Rangers fan – the only reason I married her is I felt sorry for her. I thought I'd take her to Celtic Park and show her the better things in life.

Nothing shows up the ambivalence of the Rangers–Celtic relationship so much as confrontations with the old enemy from south of the border.

COLIN GLASS   It's significant that when I started watching football the majority of Scotland fans were Rangers fans. Now I wouldn't dream of going to watch Scotland. I've got tattoos on each of my arms – one arm a Rangers tattoo, the other arm a Scotland tattoo, things that I got done when I was 18 years old. But there's no way I would go to watch Scotland now. The people who watch Scotland now tend to be Thistle fans or Aberdeen fans. Celtic fans have never watched Scotland in any great number, because their allegiances have always been to the Republic of Ireland.

EUGENE MacBRIDE   You were Ireland; but you were Scotland too. If Scotland were playing England and England won, you were heartbroken. If Scotland won then it was just ecstasy. That only broke for me one night I went to White Hart Lane, to a testimonial for John White. It was a testimonial for his widow. And I couldn't understand this – I suddenly realised that Jim Kennedy, playing left-back for Scotland, was being barracked. And then the penny dropped. Kennedy was being barracked by Rangers fans because he was a Celtic player. I think that was a watershed for me. I know that other Celtic players had to put up with this. I continued to support Scotland but I no longer felt the way I had done.

ADAM SHIELS When Celtic beat Leeds United at Hampden I stood with actual Rangers supporters – I knew, because they came from Hamilton. They were standing with us and actually shouting Celtic on, which you would never have believed, because they were playing Leeds from England. To see Rangers supporters standing and shouting Celtic on was an amazing sight.

JOHN LARKIN I used to work beside this guy who was in the Round Table – and the Round Table where I was at that time was not exactly *au fait* with Celtic and Rangers fans. They have annual conventions and that year it was in Motherwell. I forgot to tell him that that weekend Rangers were playing Celtic in Glasgow, and I didn't realise they were going up on the overnight train. An overnight train with Celtic and Rangers fans – I've been on them, they can be unbelievable. These Round Table guys were probably sitting there trying to read their papers and do their crosswords and that. My friend told me that it was hell – just running battles all night, up and down the corridor. He said that at one point the door flew open and these two guys rolled in and were fighting at their feet, rolling about on the floor, kicking hell out of each other. The Round Table guys just sat there, too scared to move. And then it stopped for a while, until, lo and behold, the word came down that there were Chelsea fans on the train . . . Chelsea were playing someone in the north the next day. And the guy said that the Rangers and Celtic fans combined to fight the Chelsea fans! That was not long ago – maybe mid-'80s.

The rest is paranoia, jokes, stupidity – anything but silence . . .

JOHN BUTTERFIELD Live football was very rare in Scotland when I was growing up. You had the Scotland–England game, the European Cup final – and that was just about that. I remember watching the 1969 Cup final very well – Billy McNeill scored that day and Alex Ferguson was playing. There's one part – Celtic are defending and Rangers break away. Greig hits a long ball. Willie Johnston nods it to Ferguson and Ferguson returns it immediately to Johnston . . . and Johnston almost hits the corner-flag. Archie MacPherson says, 'What a pathetic shot' – and by saying that, it hints fairly strongly that Archie MacPherson has some investment in seeing Rangers win. That's always the allegation – Celtic fans feel that the commentators favour Rangers.

SEAMUS MURPHY I remember one match, a Ne'erday game, I think; Rangers won 1–0. Bobby Evans miscued a ball and it went out for a shy. A Celtic wag nearby shouted out, 'That's a terrible thing for a professional player to do.' A minute or two later a Rangers player did the same thing. 'But that's bloody worse,' the same voice shouted.

GERRY MULVENNA Before the 1969 Cup final, the Rangers End was in usual form – 'The Sash' being constantly sung and the Pope being abused. A wee Glasgow man beside me at the Celtic End began hopping up and down with anger. Eventually, unable to contain himself any longer, and with the veins on his neck standing out on his forehead, he turned to me and said: 'Would you listen to that f***ing shower of foul-mouthed bastards over there!'

SUSAN AMBROSE Some of the invective that gets poured out is quite sad. At a normal League game it's usually quite funny – sarcastic, but funny. It's never funny when it comes to the Old Firm games. I remember going to Hampden for the Skol Cup game. We'd just come back from Red Star Belgrade, a 3–0 defeat, and when we got there all the Celtic fans were holding up red stars to rub it in. In normal time it was 1–1 and it went to extra time; the Rangers fans were a bit worried because they'd just come back from Europe and they thought they might be tired; in fact they rallied and they won. But during the game there was an incident right in front of where I was standing. Paul Elliott, who was playing for Celtic at the time, managed to trip up Nigel Spackman or somebody like that. And this fan right in front of me absolutely launched himself into this tirade of abuse against Paul Elliott. The upshot was – all the usual swearwords – he said: 'You're no even a real black! You're not even a real darkie! At least we've got a proper nigger! Mark Walters is black! You're just coffee-coloured!' I thought, 'My God! We're even comparing them on the colour chart . . . we've got a better black man than you because he's a slight shade darker . . .' It was really pathetic.

ANDY COTTINGHAM 6 May 1967. Celtic were playing Rangers at Ibrox in a league match; we had only to draw to win the League that year. I had three tickets for the Centenary stand which was not a bad seat. I had arranged to meet my brothers-in-law at the Five Ways pub and we had a few beers. At quarter to two we decided we should leave as we were going to the game by the subway. Outside the pub it was raining hard – a cloud-burst – and at the subway we found a sign saying that the subway was out of order due to severe flooding. Eddy went off home, but John and I rushed to try for a taxi. The queue was a mile long. We tried at Queen Street with the same result. We ran to St Enoch's; it was now 2.15 and we were panicking. Wondering what to do I noticed a young chap sitting at the wheel of a small station-wagon type car with a Rangers scarf around his neck. I said to John, 'I'm going to ask this chap if he'll give us a lift.' 'But Andy,' said John, 'they're Rangers support-ers.' 'Leave it to me,' I said, 'we're not wearing any colours.'

I approached the chap and asked him if there was any chance of a lift to the game. He said he was waiting for his mates to come out of the pub and he would see if we could be squeezed in. As an afterthought he said, 'Are you Rangers supporters?' I replied, 'I wouldn't be asking if I wasn't one of the boys.' His pals came out with a carry-out; the driver said, 'Here are two of the boys who are stranded.' They agreed to give us a lift and they squeezed John into the back. As I was reasonably big they allowed me to squeeze into the passenger seat with one of them sitting in my lap. To alleviate any doubts as to who we were, I said to the driver, 'We'll do these Fenian bastards today all right,' and started to sing 'The Sash', 'The Lily of King Billy' and the like. On arrival at the ground they parked the car, shook hands with us both and expressed their hopes that they – Rangers –

would stop these Fenian bastards winning the League. They commended me especially for being a true blue and gave us a can of lager.

GERRY DEVLIN One of my son Martin's wee pals is a Rangers fan and he kept saying to Martin, 'Get a Rangers strip, get a Rangers strip.' We said, 'No, no.' Eventually Martin said, 'Can I get a France strip?' We went to mass on a Saturday evening and the local clergyman down there is – like ninety per cent of the Catholic clergy around here – a Celtic supporter. And Martin comes in this night to six o'clock mass in blue and white . . . the priest nearly fell off the pulpit!

HUGH FERRIE There were always priests in the stand, because Celtic never charged people with clerical collars on. There was a man called Robert Jack, a great Celtic supporter. And he went to Iceland and married and became a minister in the Icelandic church. When he came back to Scotland he went back to Celtic Park, and got through with his clerical collar, you know – the Church of Iceland, or something like that!

Rangers, up until recently, gave season tickets to all the Catholic parish priests round about Ibrox. St Saviour's, St Constantine's, Lourdes. Isn't that amazing? There was a Father Fletcher who used to go every Saturday to Ibrox; he was parish priest of St Antony's, Govan. There was a Father Thompson who was a Rangers supporter because he was born in the Copland Road. If he wasn't at Ibrox people would say, 'Where's Father Thompson?'

STUART DANIELS I went with regular mates and with my father to games. I broke my ankle in 1960 at Parkhead. Rangers scored the winner in the last minute and I just remember all these bodies lying on top of me. My father came round the track with me into the ambulance room and pointed out Jimmy McGrory, the Celtic manager. He said, 'There's the Celtic manager, son. Look at his face! Rangers won the day!' He wasn't too concerned about my ankle.

DAVID POTTER   At the 1966 Cup final, a friend who couldn't get a ticket for his own end had to come to our end. He held his tongue, kept his scarf in his pocket and was relieved to see the game end 0–0. Years later while we recalled this experience, one of my friends speculated on what would have happened if his scarf had fallen out of his pocket and everybody had started kicking him. 'We would have had to kick him tae,' we decided.

JOHN LARKIN   A Celtic–Rangers final, sometime in the '50s; maybe the early '60s. It was my first Cup final – I was about 12. My dad was a taxi driver; the guy next to me was a Rangers fan, my dad said, but a really nice bloke. Stevie Chalmers scored and I jumped up. 'Sorry,' I said. Then Rangers equalised; Jimmy Millar with a header. He jumped up. 'Sorry,' he said.

DAVID POTTER   There was a chap in Forfar who supported Celtic and earned himself the nickname 'Celtic' Miller, so much so that nobody seemed to know his real name – I think it was Alec, but I'm not sure. Then, round about 1961, he got fed up with bad results and changed to supporting Rangers, but still retained his nickname. He went with friends to see the 1962 Cup final, Rangers–St Mirren, all dressed in blue. At one point he got separated from his friends, who had to shout for him. And what did they shout? 'Celtic!' It earned a few funny looks at the Mount Florida end.

One certainty remains; nothing is so comfortable, so pleasurable, as the discomfort of your main rivals.

BILL McARTHUR   The one that sticks in my mind was when Rangers were at Ibrox – I can't remember who we were playing – and Celtic were at Hampden playing Partick Thistle in the League Cup final. And when the half-time score came through, that Partick Thistle were leading Celtic 4–0, we all trooped out and got taxis and went to Hampden to see Thistle beat Celtic 4–1!

DAVID POTTER   I was at the game in 1982 when Celtic won the League against St Mirren; that tells you something about

Celtic and Rangers. Celtic had just to get a point against St Mirren; if they didn't and Aberdeen beat Rangers 4–0 Aberdeen would win the League. At half-time it was 0–0 at Parkhead, everything was tense and so on; and the half-time score on the transistors, repeated over the public address system, was Aberdeen 4, Rangers 0. And to my amazement, everybody started to cheer. They wanted the Dons to pile in more. For one day at least you'd have thought they would be hoping for Rangers to pull something back.

ANDY ROBERTSON   There's a lot of things I could tell you that you couldn't put in your book, about the boys and that, because see if their wives found out? They'd go f***ing mental. See when we went to Amsterdam . . .